T0219973

Mastering Ubuntu

Mastering Ubuntu helps the reader learn the ropes in Ubuntu for a faster and robust computing experience.

Ubuntu is a free Linux OS created by the Canonical community. It is highly customizable and features a Software Center full of apps, in addition to being open source.

Ubuntu is one of the most popular distributions due to its simplicity. It has found good traction among universities and research groups because it combines all of the functionality of a UNIX OS with a customized graphical user interface.

But just because it is free doesn't mean Ubuntu lacks the bells and whistles. It has every ingredient that a successful operating system should have, including desktop apps for a variety of purposes, such as:

- Support for all the modern web browsers, including Chrome, Firefox, Edge, and Opera

- Office and productivity apps

- Video players, audio players, and multimedia apps

- A slick and intuitive user interface

- Regularly patched security updates and bug fixes

- A robust and reliable development cycle

Ubuntu is ideal for beginners and advanced users alike. Regardless of skillset, users can quickly get to speed with Ubuntu Linux for everyday usage. This is where *Mastering Ubuntu* comes in.

With *Mastering Ubuntu*, using Ubuntu for day-to-day computing becomes a charm. This book will help readers undoubtedly boost their productivity.

The *Mastering Computer Science* series is edited by Sufyan bin Uzayr, a writer and educator with more than a decade of experience in the computing field.

Mastering Computer Science

Series Editor: Sufyan bin Uzayr

Mastering Ubuntu: A Beginner's Guide
Jaskiran Kaur, Rubina Salafey, and Shahryar Raz

Mastering React: A Beginner's Guide
Mohammad Ammar, Divya Sachdeva, and Rubina Salafey

Mastering React Native: A Beginner's Guide
Lokesh Pancha, Jaskiran Kaur, and Divya Sachdeva

Mastering Bootstrap: A Beginner's Guide
Lokesh Pancha, Divya Sachdeva, and Rubina Salafey

Mastering NativeScript: A Beginner's Guide
Divya Sachdeva, D Nikitenko and Aruqqa Khateib

Mastering GoLang: A Beginner's Guide
Divya Sachdeva, D Nikitenko, and Aruqqa Khateib

For more information about this series, please visit: https://www.routledge.com/Mastering-Computer-Science/book-series/MCS

The "Mastering Computer Science" series of books are authored by the Zeba Academy team members, led by Sufyan bin Uzayr.

Zeba Academy is an EdTech venture that develops courses and content for learners primarily in STEM fields, and offers education consulting to Universities and Institutions worldwide. For more info, please visit https://zeba.academy

Mastering Ubuntu

A Beginner's Guide

Edited by Sufyan bin Uzayr

CRC Press
Taylor & Francis Group
Boca Raton London New York

CRC Press is an imprint of the
Taylor & Francis Group, an **informa** business

First Edition published 2023
by CRC Press
6000 Broken Sound Parkway NW, Suite 300, Boca Raton, FL 33487-2742

and by CRC Press
2 Park Square, Milton Park, Abingdon, Oxon, OX14 4RN

CRC Press is an imprint of Taylor & Francis Group, LLC

© 2023 Sufyan bin Uzayr

Library of Congress Cataloging-in-Publication Data

Names: Bin Uzayr, Sufyan, editor.
Title: Mastering Ubuntu : a beginner's guide / edited by Sufyan bin Uzayr.
Description: First edition. | Boca Raton : CRC Press, 2023. | Series:
  Mastering computer science
Identifiers: LCCN 2022020966 (print) | LCCN 2022020967 (ebook) | ISBN
  9781032319094 (hardback) | ISBN 9781032319070 (paperback) | ISBN
  9781003311997 (ebook)
Subjects: LCSH: Ubuntu (Electronic resource) | Linux. | Operating systems
  (Computers)
Classification: LCC QA76.774.U28 .M37 2023 (print) | LCC QA76.774.U28
  (ebook) | DDC 005.4/32--dc23/eng/20220815
LC record available at https://lccn.loc.gov/2022020966
LC ebook record available at https://lccn.loc.gov/2022020967

ISBN: 9781032319094 (hbk)
ISBN: 9781032319070 (pbk)
ISBN: 9781003311997 (ebk)

DOI: 10.1201/ 9781003311997

Typeset in Minion
by Deanta Global Publishing Services, Chennai, India

Contents

Mastering Computer Science Series Preface

THE *MASTERING COMPUTER SCIENCE* covers a wide range of topics, spanning programming languages as well as modern-day technologies and frameworks. The series has a special focus on beginner-level content, and is presented in an easy to understand manner, comprising:

- Crystal-clear text, spanning various topics sorted by relevance

- Special focus on practical exercises, with numerous code samples and programs

- A guided approach to programming, with step by step tutorials for the absolute beginners

- Keen emphasis on real-world utility of skills, thereby cutting the redundant and seldom-used concepts and focusing instead of industry-prevalent coding paradigm

- A wide range of references and resources, to help both beginner and intermediate-level developers gain the most out of the books

The *Mastering Computer Science* series of books start from the core concepts, and then quickly move on to industry-standard coding practices, to help learners gain efficient and crucial skills in as little time as possible. The books assume no prior knowledge of coding, so even the absolute newbie coders can benefit from this series.

The *Mastering Computer Science* series is edited by Sufyan bin Uzayr, a writer and educator with more than a decade of experience in the computing field.

About the Editor

Sufyan bin Uzayr is a writer, coder, and entrepreneur with more than a decade of experience in the industry. He has authored several books in the past, pertaining to a diverse range of topics, ranging from history to computers/IT.

Sufyan is the Director of Parakozm, a multinational IT company specializing in EdTech solutions. He also runs Zeba Academy, an online learning and teaching vertical with a focus on STEM fields.

Sufyan specializes in a wide variety of technologies, such as JavaScript, Dart, WordPress, Drupal, Linux, and Python. He holds multiple degrees, including ones in management, IT, literature, and political science.

Sufyan is a digital nomad, dividing his time between four countries. He has lived and taught in universities and educational institutions around the globe. Sufyan takes a keen interest in technology, politics, literature, history, and sports, and in his spare time, he enjoys teaching coding and English to young students.

Learn more at sufyanism.com.

CHAPTER 1

Introduction to Ubuntu

IN THIS CHAPTER

- ➤ Linux
- ➤ UNIX Origins and History
- ➤ Distribution
- ➤ History of Ubuntu
- ➤ Ubuntu flavors
- ➤ Features
- ➤ Advantages and disadvantages
- ➤ The Ubuntu Community and Goals
- ➤ Canonical and the Ubuntu Foundation
- ➤ Ubuntu Desktop
- ➤ Ubuntu Server

In this chapter, we will briefly talk about Ubuntu's working, foundation, history, features, advantages, and disadvantages with its different flavors.

DOI: 10.1201/9781003311997-1

UBUNTU

Ubuntu Linux is one of several variants, and it is also referred to as distributions of the Linux operating system and is a U.K. company named Canonical Ltd. In 1994, the company was founded by Mark Shuttleworth. This chapter will give you knowledge of the Linux operating system and Ubuntu history.

It also defines the history of Ubuntu throughout its past and looks to its future. If you are looking for installation, you can jump right in and get started with Ubuntu, and you can even miss this and proceed immediately to Chapter 2, Installing Ubuntu. Start with this chapter if you want to learn more about Ubuntu's origins and future plans.

UNIX ORIGINS

To understand the history of Linux O.S., we first have to go to AT&T Bell Laboratories in the 1960s. AT&T had finished developing a new operating system named Multics during this time. The Two AT&T creators, Ken Thompson and Dennis Ritchie, chose to take what they had discovered from the Multics project and create a new operating system called UNIX which quickly achieved popularity and vast adoption with corporations and academic institutions.

A variety of UNIX implementations finally came to market, including those created by (AIX) IBM, (HP-UX), Hewlett-Packard, and (SunOS and Solaris) Sun Microsystems. In extra, a UNIX-based operating system named MINIX was designed by Andrew S. Tanenbaum invented for educational use with code access provided to universities.

WHO CREATED LINUX?

The fundamental origins of Linux can be traced back and also the philosophies of two people. The main part of the Linux operating system is called the kernel. This is the basic set of features necessary for the operating system to do something. The kernel manages the system resources and handles communication between the hardware and the applications. Linus Torvalds developed the Linux kernel. He dislikes MS-DOS, and impatient for the availability of MINIX for the new Intel 80386 microprocessor, decided to write his UNIX-like kernel. When the first version of the kernel is released under an open-source license, it enables anyone to download the source code, freely use and modify it without paying any money.

At the same time, Richard Stallman at the Free Software Foundation, a strong advocate of free and open-source software, is working on an open-source operating system of his own. However, rather than focusing initially on the kernel, Stallman decided to develop open-source versions of all the UNIX/Linux tools, utilities, compilers necessary to use and maintain an operating system. By the time he finished developing this UNIX infrastructure, it seemed like the obvious solution was to combine work with the kernel Linus had written to create an entire operating system.

This whole combination became known as GNU-Linux. The Purists insist that Linux always be referred to as GNU-Linux. This is not defined given that the GNU tools developed by the Free Software Foundation make up a significant and vital part of GNU-Linux. Most people and publications refer to Linux as Linux, which will probably continue to be the case.

WHAT IS A DISTRIBUTION?

Ubuntu is an O.S. The whole story is a little more complex. It is called a distribution of GNU/Linux. They now understand what that indicates, a little bit of history. In the early days, GNU and Linux, the users needed a great deal of technical knowledge. Only things are required to apply. There was a set of disks that one could install. The software was hundreds of individual programs, each built differently by a different and distributed separately.

By installing each of the necessary applications would be incredibly time-consuming at best. In most cases, incompatibilities and the technical trickery required to install software made getting a GNU/Linux system on a hard disk prohibitively tricky. A great configuration and programming knowledge was needed to get a system up and running. Few people who are not programmers use these GNU/Linux systems now.

Early distributions collected all of the necessary pieces of software from all of the different places. They put them together in an easier-to-install form with the most basic configuration already done.

These distributions aimed to make using GNU/Linux more convenient and more effective for users. Today, almost nobody uses GNU/Linux without using a distribution. As a result, distribution names are well known. Ubuntu is a project, and other popular distros include Red Hat and Fedora, Novell's SUSE, Gentoo, and Debian.

The relationship between Ubuntu and Debian is not simple, straightforward, or painless and has patience and learning on both sides. While the association has yet to be perfected, with time, it has improved consistently, and both groups have found ways to work together that seem to offer significant benefits over the traditional derive-and-forget model. Through a complex set of technological and other processes described in the rest of this chapter, Ubuntu tries to create a better way to build a free software distribution.

THE DEBIAN AND THE FREE SOFTWARE

Debian is distributed by a volunteer of many hundreds of official members, more volunteers, and contributors and expanded to encompass over 30,000 free and open source applications and documentation packages. Debian's history and structure make it very good at certain things. For example, Debian has a well-known reputation for package management and access to an extensive list of free software applications. However, a voluntary and largely non-hierarchical Debian had a challenging time providing frequent and reliable releases, corporate support and liability, and a top-down consistency.

WHAT IS GNU/LINUX?

Linux is a series of programs that interact with your computer and run other programs.

A system consists of various basic programs your computer needs to communicate and get instructions, such as read and writing data to hard disks. The printer also controls memory use and runs other software. The critical part of a system is the kernel. In a GNU-Linux system, Linux is the kernel component. The system consists of other programs written by the GNU Project. The Linux kernel does not form a working operating system alone, then prefers to use the specific term "GNU/Linux." It refers to techniques that many people casually refer to as "Linux."

Linux is based on the Unix operating system and designed to be a multi-tasking, multi-user system from the start. These facts make Linux different from other well-known operating systems. However, Linux is even more diverse. Nobody owns Linux because much of its development is done by unpaid volunteers, unlike other operating systems.

The Free Software Foundation started a free Unix-like operating system called GNU. It has created a comprehensive set of free software tools with Unix-like operating systems such as Linux. These tools enable to perform tasks ranging from the mundane to the arcane.

Linux is a minor crash, better able to run more than one program simultaneously, and more secure than many operating systems. Linux is the fastest-growing operating system in the server market with these advantages. More recently, Linux began to be popular among home and business users.

GUI ALTERNATIVES

The default environment of Ubuntu is GNOME. It runs fine on the majority of hardware. Still, suppose you're working with a particularly low-spec computer or virtual environment. In that case, you can use a different desktop interface that has been optimized to use fewer system resources than GNOME does.

Xubuntu is a lightweight desktop system or the even more lightweight Lubuntu. Both of these desktop environments will use fewer system resources than GNOME. They look slightly different, and some prefer them even if their system can run GNOME just fine.

THE HISTORY OF UBUNTU

Ubuntu is one of the important Linux distributions. Its source code that makes up the Ubuntu distribution originates from a highly regarded Linux distribution known as Debian, created by Ian Murdoch.

Mark Shuttleworth, a South African internet mogul, decided it was time for a more user-friendly Linux. Then he took the Debian distribution and worked to make it a more human-friendly distribution called Ubuntu and subsequently formed a company called Canonical Ltd to promote and support Ubuntu.

If you are new or already use Linux and want to try a different Linux distribution, you will unlikely find a better option than Ubuntu.

Year by year, Ubuntu has continued to mature. The public notice of Ubuntu with Ubuntu 6.06 LTS, the first release with long-term support for both desktops and servers, followed by a new release every six months and a new release LTS release every two years up to the current 12.04 LTS. Ubuntu proves it intends to stick around long-term while improving consistently and on a predictable schedule with these releases. With this maturation, the project maintains its vigor, ambitious attitude, commitment to its principles, and community-driven approach. As the project ages, it proves that it can learn from its failures and successes and maintain growth without compromising stability.

WHAT DOES THE WORD "UBUNTU" MEAN?

"Ubuntu" is an old Zulu and Xhosa word that means "humanity to others." Ubuntu OS also means "I am what I am because of who we all are" because these opinions exactly describe the core of the Ubuntu distribution.

Ubuntu is an open and free operating system that competes with commercially available proprietary operating systems like Windows and macOS. A panel shows the time, indicators, and a way to open an overview of the screen or dashboard that accesses your apps. You can switch between windows and virtual desktops.

The company behind Ubuntu is called Canonical. Instead, Ubuntu is the free and open-source component that comes from teams from all over the world. A desktop environment is known as GNOME.

Canonical Foundation uses these components to create a desktop experience that anyone can download. You can use Ubuntu for your general computing, office work, and gaming, software development. Also, you can use Ubuntu to run servers.

ARE UBUNTU AND LINUX THE SAME?

The kernel is the part that enables software to talk to your computer's hardware in Linux. The Linux kernel is one of many components. Canonical Foundation used to create the Ubuntu desktop.

Linux and Ubuntu are that you can't run the kernel (Linux) independently. It runs in the background, powering many devices, such as gas station pumps to Android smartphones. The Desktop is less about Linux and more concerning for all the free and open-source software. That said, it is more accurate to think of Ubuntu as Ubuntu Linux than as its own separate thing.

The Ubuntu Infrastructure

Ubuntu is more significant than the Desktop. You can Ubuntu download it from its official site name ubuntu.com. It has a massive community of developers and users. It also has a collection of apps and programs gathered from many sources and used differently.

It is based on Debian, a vast project that does the same thing in Ubuntu, but it is less accessible. To clear items up, we will have to establish a few terms.

The way developers differentiate software for Linux Apps, components of the system, drivers, codecs, and various software come in containers called packages.

Package: The different versions of Linux organize packages using other formats. As of yet, there's no single format that's compatible with every version of Linux.

Repositories in Linux software are usually found in a repository instead of downloading installers from a website. Repositories are extensive collections of packages that you may access and download as needed.

A distribution is a collection of software packaged to provide a functioning operating system and the accompanying community and repositories.

Ubuntu and Debian are both Linux distributions, and Ubuntu uses the same DEB package format as Debian, though the software isn't always compatible. Ubuntu provides its repositories, but it mostly fills them with packages from Debian.

BEFORE YOU BEGIN THE INSTALLATION

Installing a new operating system is a most significant event, and you should make sure that you have properly thought about what is going to occur. However, Ubuntu runs well on various hardware, and it is valuable to check your hardware components because some bits of hardware do not work well with Ubuntu.

This portion provides some areas for you to investigate and think about; it might save you hours of frustration when something goes wrong, and problems are becoming much less frequent, but they still crop up occasionally.

You can start by researching and documenting your hardware. This information will prove helpful later on during the installation.

At the absolute, you should know the basics of your system, such as how much RAM you have, what type of mouse, keyboard; knowing the storage capacity, kind of hard drive you have is crucial because it helps you plan how to divide it for Ubuntu and troubleshoot if problems occur. Whether your mouse uses the USB, a small detail ensures proper pointer configuration something should happen without any problem, but you will be glad you know it if something goes wrong. The other information you have, the better prepared you are for any issues.

Again, the items you most want to know to include the amount of installed memory, the size of your hard drive, the type of mouse, the capabilities of the display monitor, and the number of installed network interfaces.

WHAT ARE THE VARIOUS KINDS OF UBUNTU AVAILABLE?

In Desktop Linux, the desktop variants are also referred to as 'flavors.' Below is the list of official Ubuntu flavors:

Ubuntu GNOME (default Ubuntu flavor)

- **Default Ubuntu (Ubuntu GNOME):** Ubuntu Desktop and Ubuntu Server are both available in the default version. The following are the main changes between these two versions:

  - The desktop environment is included in the Ubuntu Desktop edition, which is not included in the Ubuntu Server distribution.

  - When installing Ubuntu Server, a command-line interface is used, whereas Ubuntu Desktop employs a graphical user interface.

  - The default setup of Ubuntu Desktop is automatically tailored for desktop usage, whereas the server edition is designed for server use.

  The Ubuntu kernel was separately optimized for both versions, including their support lifecycles. From version 12.04 onward, both editions are the same, except for their default installation configurations.

- **Xubuntu:** It's a lite version of Ubuntu. The desktop variation is the main distinction between Xubuntu and Lubuntu. Xubuntu utilises Xfce, a fast, "lightweight desktop environment for UNIX-like operating systems," whereas Lubuntu uses LDXE. It does not consume a lot of system resources and is visually pleasing, user-friendly, and efficient. Users may, for example, right-click anywhere on the Desktop to bring up the start menu.

  Also, It is more configurable than Lubuntu, featuring business-ready apps such as LibreOffice contained in the standard installation.

- **Lubuntu:** The Lubuntu describes itself as a "fast and lightweight operating system with a clean and easy-to-use user interface." It is the third most popular Ubuntu flavour and runs on the LXDE desktop, which was launched in 2006.

  It has low hardware needs because to its simple desktop, lightweight operating system, and lightweight apps.

- **Kubuntu:** It is the second most popular flavor. First released in 2005, It uses the KDE desktop by default.

  It is well-known for having a desktop experience that is comparable to that of Windows. It not only has a start button and taskbar like Windows, but it also has the most customization options of any Linux desktop. However, there is one disadvantage to this customization capability: it depletes system resources. In other words, it consumes a lot of system resources, therefore installing it on an older machine or one with limited memory and CPU resources is not a smart idea.

- **Ubuntu Mate:** This flavor is structured around the MATE desktop environment. In other terms, the fact is that there is a user requirement for the MATE desktop. When Ubuntu changed from Unity to GNOME as its default desktop, MATE was born. However, rather than matching the GNOME 2 desktop with Ubuntu's default version (Ubuntu GNOME), Ubuntu chose to create a new or unique version of GNOME. GNOME 2 enthusiasts were not pleased, hence Ubuntu MATE was created.

- **Ubuntu Budgie:** Jack Wallen describes Ubuntu Budgie as the "new kid on the block." It has the Budgie desktop and a modern, appealing user interface. In the overview, this Ubuntu flavor suggests a current, lightweight, fast operating system with an elegant desktop interface, suitable for use on any device from an old workstation to the latest Desktop or laptop. It is also not extremely complicated.

  Lastly, this variant was originally created by the Ubuntu community. It was later formed as an official Ubuntu flavor and released in 2016.

- **Ubuntu Kylin:** Ubuntu Kylin is the official version of Ubuntu. It is more than just language localization. It is determined to serve the Chinese market the same way Ubuntu does the global market.

  The first version of Kylin came with Ubuntu 13.04. Like Ubuntu, Kylin has LTS long-term support and non-LTS versions.

  Ubuntu Kylin LTS implements the UKUI desktop environment with revised boot-up animation, log-in/screen-lock, and O.S. theme. To offer a better experience for users, it has fixed bugs, a file function, timer log-out, the WPS office suite, and Sogou put-in methods.

Kylin is a community edition based on Ubuntu Kylin LTS. It includes several third-party applications with long-term and stable support. It is perfect for server and desktop usage for daily office work and welcomes developers to download. The Kylin forums are actively available to provide feedback and troubleshoot to find solutions.

- **Ubuntu Studio:** The main difference between these Ubuntu flavors is the desktop variant packaged with the default installation. One of the intended results of the default desktop is either high configurability at the cost of system resource usage or an extremely lightweight, fast flavor that is low on resources.

  Besides, Ubuntu Studio uses the Xfce desktop environment. In this matter, the performance specifications are higher because of this flavor's planned practical usage. Ubuntu Studio is packaged with preinstalled video and audio tools. These tools are appropriate and required for non-professionals and individuals wanting to create and edit audio, video, and graphics files.

- **Edubuntu:** It is a product of Ubuntu desired for educational use and schools. To install Edubuntu, you should first install the default desktop version of Ubuntu, then use either the downloadable add-on Edubuntu CD or the Ubuntu Software Center in Applications menu on the Desktop to install the Edubuntu environment and applications.

We specifically mentioned that these are the 'official' flavors. Canonical, Ubuntu's parent company, endorses these flavors. They release a new version simultaneously as the main Ubuntu supports default GNOME edition releases. They follow the same cycle of development and release schedule.

Ubuntu comes in a variety of flavors. In this, we briefly discussed some of the popular tastes of Ubuntu.

- **Ubuntu Desktop:** This is the operating system that regular users can use. It comes pre-built with software that helps the users perform usual basic activities. It has various operations such as browsing, email, and multimedia are available in this version. The latest version of 2016 is 16.04.01.

- **Ubuntu Server:** The Ubuntu server version is used for hosting web servers and databases applications. Ubuntu has supported each server version for five years. These systems support cloud platforms such as AWS and Azure. The latest version as of 2016 is 16.04.1.

- **Kubuntu:** The Ubuntu standard interface is based on software known as Unity. Hence, It is based on a software called KDE Plasma desktop. It gives a different look and feels to the Ubuntu software. It has the same features and software availability as Ubuntu. The official site for Kubuntu

FEATURES

The following are some of the significant features of Ubuntu:

- The desktop version supports all the usual software on Windows, such as Firefox, Chrome, and VLC.
- It supports the office suite called LibreOffice.
- It has an in-built email software called Thunderbird, which gives users access to Exchange, Gmail, Hotmail, etc.
- There are many free applications for users to view and edit photos.
- There are applications to manage videos and allow users to share videos.
- It is easy to find your content on Ubuntu with an intelligent searching facility.
- The best feature is that it is a free operating system and is backed by a vast open source community.

Microsoft's Windows currently owns 90% of the market share for desktop computers, so what advantages a Linux distribution, specifically, Ubuntu over Windows.

But several features make Ubuntu a better O.S. for your workstation than Windows is.

Here is the list of the advantages of Ubuntu over Windows.

Advantages

- **Ubuntu is completely Free:** Because Ubuntu runs free, and millions of people worldwide can use affordable computers that run efficient

O.S. and properly-developed applications. Many schools that can't afford Windows computers can quickly resort to the beautiful open-source Linux distro without the fear of losing productivity, beauty, or efficiency.

- **Ubuntu is customizable:** Ubuntu is customizable whenever you install it. The latest version uses the GNOME version desktop environment, allowing you to personalize virtually every element of your UI-UX, from notification sounds, popup style, fonts, system animations, and workspaces.

- **Ubuntu Is More Secure:** Ubuntu hasn't kept many security bridges and viruses. Although Windows 10 has a good amount of security improvements. Ubuntu is not immune to safety flaws but built from its kernel up with more emphasis on operating techniques to cover for the recklessness of her not so tech-inclined users, allowing them to be a lot more helpful with their portable storage devices and accessories.

- **Ubuntu runs without installing:** It means that you can carry your OS along with your files, boot it on another workstation and carry on working as if the PC is yours.

  You do not need to wait via a whole installation process because you can run Ubuntu as Live directly from a pen drive.

- **Ubuntu is Better Suited for Development:** A Ubuntu installation comes with out-of-the-box support for users to get straight to work on projects with their machines. Before you can have a positive working environment, you'll need to install an office suite, Python, Ruby, a text editor, Java, and other programs.

  Windows can ship as a multi-purpose, multi-use product packaged. Still, Ubuntu has the advantage of providing its users with an office suite, a text editor, and various other productivity apps from the get-go, and it saves a lot of time.

- **Ubuntu Command Line:** Ubuntu comes with support for Bash in its command line as default and various other commands that make working on servers, development environments, and local files a lot easier.

- **Help and Support:** One of the things about Ubuntu Linux is the community surrounding it. Out of all the Linux distros out there, it can manage to have the best support for its users. Many will say that Ubuntu has many avenues for help because it's the most "well-known" Linux OS. Well, they're right. Many people regularly talk about Ubuntu, and that's great for the average user.

- **Excellent for Developing Unique Programs:** You can easily install Ubuntu on your device without installing any external script like python, Java, and so on. The Linux operating system is designed so that it will be easy to use after installation for programmers. If you still have any issues while running this software, use the apt-get command that will help install the software with single line code.

- **Great Options for Documentation:** If you are using Word Press for your website, then Ubuntu will benefit you. The Linux operating system is very well at its documentation. Ubuntu's search engine will help many programmers with their projects as they quickly get what they might need.

- **Update without Restarting:** Ubuntu can download updates in the background, so you'll seldom be interrupted from your work. This is one of the reasons why Windows operating systems are rarely utilized for services that require continual reading, such as web page serving.

- **Ubuntu Is Open-Source:** It is free and open-source to all, or you can go through Ubuntu source code and make the best contributions to it, which will allow you to be innovative while learning about the inner workings of an excellent OS. The same can neither be said about Windows nor macOS.

- **Solid Interface with Command Line:** Ubuntu has an excellent command-line interface that is reasonably simple to learn. Aside from that, it has other commands that make server management, using local files, and working in the development environment much more accessible.

- **Compared to Other OS Ubuntu Is Secured:** Okay, while designing a highly secured firewall for websites, Linux Ubuntu will provide frequent security updates to its software. You only need to set up an initial step after doing proper research, and then, after all this, you will be vigorously protected.

- **Ubuntu Is More Resource-Friendly:** Ubuntu runs on older hardware far better than Windows. Even Windows 10, which is more resource-friendly than its predecessors, does not do as good of a job as any Linux distro.

  Therefore, customers who cannot afford high-end laptops and desktops can install Ubuntu on their old workstations with assurance.

- **Ubuntu Supports Window Tiling:** The last but minor point is that tiling managers like herbstluftwm are best used when you have multiple monitors and allocate app positions across your monitors. Both Windows and Ubuntu feature various desktops (workspaces), but Windows does not have any tiling managers as far as I know.

- **Easy and Straightforward to Use:** Ubuntu Linux is defined as "Linux for human beings." Out of all the Linux-based operating systems available on the market today, none come close to the ease of use that Ubuntu provides and from installing complicated video drivers to getting Netflix and Hulu working on setting up a dual-boot system. With Microsoft Windows, Ubuntu is the best!

- **Long Term Support Releases:** A common only reason to avoid Linux is that it appears to be less "stable" than other systems. Worries about operating system stability are legible, but overall, Linux has come a long way; gone are the times when everything was broken and unusable.

  This Ubuntu focuses on stability and reliability. Its LTS releases are the most popular version of Ubuntu and get updates and support for up to 5 years!

- **Ubuntu Popularity:** Ubuntu is the widespread Linux distribution today. Its popularity is to the creativity and the excellent support in the Ubuntu platforms, which we all like. And it is still being improved day by day.

Disadvantages

- **Limited Functionality Due to Limited Applications:** One of the main disadvantages of Ubuntu is the small choices of applications. Although the O.S. is free and several apps are also free for download, counter-parts in Windows and macOS are much better. The professional developers also prefer developing for Microsoft Corporation and Apple Inc. because they have larger user bases.

Determinate that there are Linux choices for several famous Windows and macOS applications. However, the user interface and features or functionalities of Ubuntu are still different. Also, popular software in Windows or macOS for image and video editing, music production, and other productivity tools have become industry standards.

- **Problems about Software and Hardware Compatibility:** Some of the users have reported driver or compatibility issues between the operating system and the hardware of their computers. There have been reports of wireless card drivers not working and the printer not connecting to the computer due to some unidentified hardware problem. It is another critical disadvantage of Ubuntu.

- **You Need An Experts while Operating:** While developing any website, you will need to help some experts who are mastered in this field. They will simplify the codes, commands, and other essential functions where you may be stuck. While using any complex operating system, you may need some developers to help behind it.

- **There Are Better Linux Operating System Alternatives:** Experienced Linux users agree that Ubuntu is not the most suitable Linux distribution. Some say that the Debian operating system allows for more customization and provides a more reliable environment. It runs efficiently under a lightweight hardware configuration. Determinate that Ubuntu is based on Debian.

  Another alternative is Linux Mint. Note that this OS is a community-driven Linux distribution based on Ubuntu. It runs on a lower system. This software management is also faster, sleeker, and lighter. Customization is also straightforward. The O.S. package comes with relevant media and additional apps out of the box.

- **Not Good For Gaming:** The most significant disadvantage of the Ubuntu operating system is that you cannot entirely run any latest game on this platform. If you still want to play the game, you may need to install an emulator such as WINE or any other external software. The graphics you will get in windows are not be provided by

Ubuntu. Therefore, Ubuntu has feeble graphic support for its users. So avoid using this operating system if you are game.

- **Problem with OpenVPN vs. Commercial Source:** The most common review of Ubuntu is that it seems to be commercialized. With the release, Canonical appears to drift more away from the root of the open-source operating system. Instead of cooperating with the open-source community, the company works on its own most of the time and misses out on the benefit of free input from hundreds of developers.

- **Difficult to Migrate:** Suppose you are using a WordPress site and thinking of migrating it on a shared hosting service. In that case, you may find some difficulties while migrating it to a server hosted by the Ubuntu operating system.

- **Tough to Understand Operating:** Users who might not know about command-line programs may find difficulties while operating Ubuntu. They approach many YouTube tutorial videos to run a program in this operating system. Once they understand the whole game, it will be much easier to use Linux Ubuntu on their workstation.

- **Limited Functionality:** The main disadvantage of Ubuntu that developers experience is the limited availability of resources. As it's open-source and many apps are free to download, but this option is much better in other O.S. like Windows and macOS.

- **Hardware and Software Complications:** Many of the users reported that they might experience driver issues. This problem is occurring on the software and hardware of the O.S. of their device. They see major trouble connecting any wireless devices or printers because of hardware issues.

- **MP3 Format Is Restricted:** If you are a video editor, you may find difficulty working on Ubuntu for your work. O.S. like Windows doesn't require any external codes to run a video, but you may need to add such applications or codes in Ubuntu.

Therefore, we have discussed all the significant advantages and disadvantages of Ubuntu, and many active users have noted the drawbacks as mentioned above of Ubuntu.

- **The Ubuntu Community:** Ubuntu might not be what it is now without the Ubuntu community. Even the definition of Ubuntu revolves around people interacting in a community. The following chapters will discuss the Ubuntu community, organized, and how those who choose can get involved.

UBUNTU PROMISES AND GOALS

So far, this chapter has been about the prehistory, history, and context of the Ubuntu project. This book will now concentrate on the distribution itself. Before proceeding, it's essential to understand the goals that motivated the project.

PHILOSOPHICAL GOALS

The essential goals of the Ubuntu project are philosophical. The Ubuntu project lays out the philosophy in documents Ubuntu Promises and Goals on its Website. The team summarizes this chapter and the primary intellectual goals and underpinnings in the most central of these documents.

1. **Our Philosophy:** Our work philosophy of software freedom aims to spread and bring software benefits to all parts of the world. At the core of it is Philosophy are these core ideas:

   - Each computer user has the freedom to download, run, copy, share, change, distribute, study, and improve their software for another purpose without paying licensing fees.

   - Each computer user should use their software in the language of their choice.

   - Each computer user should be given every opportunity to use software, even if they work under a disability.

   Our philosophy in the software we produce and included in our distribution. As an outcome, the licensing terms of the software we distribute are measured against our philosophy, using the Ubuntu License Policy.

   When you install Ubuntu, almost all software installed already meets these ideals. We ensure that every piece of software you need is available under a license that gives you freedom.

Currently, we make a particular exception for some "drivers" that are available only in binary form. Without many computers, it will not complete the Ubuntu installation. We place that these in a restricted section of your system, making them easy to remove if you do not need them.

2. **Free Software:** For Ubuntu, it is used primarily about freedom and not to price. However, we have not committed any charges for Ubuntu. The important thing about Ubuntu is that it grants software freedom rights to the people who install and use it to enable the Ubuntu community to grow and continue sharing its experience and expertise. It helps to improve Ubuntu and make it suitable for use in all new countries and industries.

   - The freedom to run the program

   - The freedom to learn the program working

   - The freedom to redistribute copies so which can help others

   - Improve the program and release their improvements to the others so that everyone benefits

3. **Open-Source:** Open source is a term started in 1998 to remove the ambiguity in the English word free. The Open Source described open-source software in the Open Source Definition. Open-source continues to appreciate growing success and wide recognition.

   Ubuntu calls itself open-source, while others refer to free and open source as competing movements with different ends. We do not see free and open-source software as distinct or incompatible. It proudly includes members who identify with both activities.

   The main goals of Ubuntu don't end with the free software definition. As a result, Ubuntu is the project and community responsibility of Ubuntu Promises and Goals to ensure that every user can use Ubuntu to read and write in the most familiar language with comfortable.

CONDUCT GOALS AND CODE OF CONDUCT

Ubuntu's CoC is, arguably, an essential document in the day-to-day operation of the Ubuntu community, setting some ground rules for work and cooperation within the project. The document's explicit agreement is the only criterion for becoming an officially recognized Ubuntu activist – an Ubuntu – and is essential to membership in the project.

The CoC covers "its manners as a member of the Ubuntu community, in any forum, mailing list, wiki, Web site, IRC channel, install-fest, etc." The CoC goes into depth on a series of points under the following headings:

- Be considerate.

- Be respectful.

- Be collaborative.

- When you disagree, you should consult others.

- When you are unsure, you should ask for help.

SUSTAINING THE VISION

Canonical and the Ubuntu Foundation

A community drives Ubuntu, and several groups play an essential role in its structure and organization. Canonical, Ltd., a for-profit company introduced as part of the Ubuntu record description and the Ubuntu Foundation, is presented later in this section.

About Canonical

It is the publisher of Ubuntu, the operating system for public cloud workloads and the emerging categories of intelligent gateways, self-driving cars, and advanced robots. It provides enterprise security, support, and services to commercial users of Ubuntu. Established in 2004, Canonical is a privately held company.

Canonical, Ltd.

Canonical, Ltd. was founded by Mark Shuttleworth to develop and support the Ubuntu distribution. Core developers on Ubuntu are no longer a majority of Sustaining the Vision: Canonical and the Ubuntu Foundation they work full time or part-time as Canonical, Ltd. This funding allows Ubuntu to make support commitments. As an all-volunteer organization, Debian suffered from an inability to set and meet deadlines. Volunteers become busy or have deadlines in their paying jobs that take precedence.

Canonical has announced the Ubuntu Frame, a simple solution that allows developers to quickly build and deploy graphical applications for interactive kiosks, digital signage solutions, or any other products that Canonical's Ubuntu Frame is an easy-to-use, reliable, and secure fullscreen shell to power edge devices, with ten years of support from Canonical.

With Ubuntu Frame, the developers have no longer need to integrate and maintain partial DRM, KMS, input protocols, or security policies to power and secure their displays. This means less code to manage, fewer opportunities for bugs and vulnerabilities in code, and extra time for developing the content.

This Frame makes it easier for customers to create customizable, reliable, and more secure smart retail and digital signage solutions.

Ubuntu is incomplete without introducing a growing list of Ubuntu subprojects and derivatives where the Ubuntu was derived from Debian. That project has also developed several derivatives.

First among these is Kubuntu, a version of Ubuntu that uses KDE instead of GNOME as the default desktop environment. The relationship between Kubuntu and Ubuntu is different from that between Ubuntu and Debian. From a technical perspective, Kubuntu is entirely within the Ubuntu distribution. The Kubuntu team works completely within Ubuntu as well.

WHAT IS KDE IN LINUX?

KDE stands for K Desktop Environment. It is a desktop environment for Linux-based operating systems. You can think of KDE as a GUI for Linux O.S. KDE has proved Linux users to make its use as easy as they use windows. KDE provides Linux users a graphical interface to choose their customized desktop environment. You can select your Graphical Interface among various available GUI interfaces with their look.

You can imagine Linux without KDE and GNOME, just like DOS in windows. KDE and GNOME are similar to Windows, except they are related to Linux through x server rather than an operating system. When you install Linux, you choose your desktop environment from two or three different desktop environments like KDE and GNOME. Another popular environment, same as KDE, is GNOME.

WHAT IS GNOME?

GNOME (pronounced gah-NOHM), a graphical user interface (GUI) stands for (GNU Network Object Model Environment), and set of computer desktop applications for users of the Linux operating system. It intended to make a Linux operating system easy for non-programmers and generally corresponds to the Windows desktop interface and its most common set of applications. It allows the user to select several desktop appearances. With GNOME, the user interface can, for example, be made to look like Windows or like Mac OS.

DIFFERENCES BETWEEN UBUNTU AND WINDOWS 10

What Is Ubuntu?

It is open-source software that was developed by Canonical in October 2004. It is a very reliable operating system. Its latest release is Ubuntu 18.10. It comes with three official editions:

- **Ubuntu Desktop**: It is for the personal computer

- **Ubuntu Server**: It is for making the servers

- **Ubuntu Core**: It is for the IoT and Robots.

Some features of Ubuntu are given below:

- It is an open-source operating system.

- It has a better User Interface.

- According to a security point of view, It is very safe because it's less valuable, and the font family in Ubuntu is very much better than windows.

- It has a centralized software Repository from which we can download all required software from that.

- Its Unix Environment is the best for the programmer.

- It has a command-line interface and the GUI interface.

- It's open-source, which is free of charge.

What Is Windows 10?

Windows 10 is an operating system that Microsoft developed and was released in July 2015 to target personal computing.

The features of Window 10 are given below:

- Windows 10 is the latest version and the best update of the Windows series.

- It is the best Operating system for gamers.

- The U.I. interface of Windows 10 is excellent.

- It supports many apps, and keyboard and mouse attractions are very nice.

- We can easily sync our windows mobile with the Windows 10 operating system.

- It has a Cortana, a personal visual assistant that is very useful and helpful.

- It has a new browser name as Microsoft edge.

- It has a better snap assist.

Comparison between Ubuntu and Windows

Developer	Canonical	Microsoft
O.S. Family	Linux	Windows
Source Model	Open Source	Licensed
Release	20-October-2004	15-July-2015
Kernel	Type Monolithic	Hybrid
Userland	GNU	Windows NT,.NET
Default User Interface	GNOME, Ubuntu Unity	Windows Shell
Cost	Free	Open-source, Paid, Licensed version
Viruses	It can't survive	It attaches is common
Updates	Updates are very easy	Every time you need to update the Java
Programming	The programming part is very easy	It is comfortable but not much compatible.
Entertainment	It is not built for entertainment	All movies, songs, and photos are very handy

(Continued)

Developer	Canonical	Microsoft
MS Office work	It is comfortable with MS Office	It works excellent in Windows
Gaming	You can play games in Ubuntu	Windows will support all ALI games
Photoshop and Adobe support	It is not supported	It works very well.
Performance of	RAM is better than windows	Okay in windows
Security	No need for Antivirus and Firewall	It always needs one
Learning	It is not easy to learn	It is very easy to learn.

UBUNTU APPS

Ubuntu is widely regarded as a beginner-friendly version of Linux, but that doesn't mean that Beginners only use Ubuntu. Advanced users can also use some of the great features Ubuntu has to offer.

WHAT IS APT?

APT stands for Advanced Package Tool. The clue is the name. It's a command-line tool for managing packages within Ubuntu.

Ubuntu is based on the Debian operating system. It makes use of the DPKG package manager, which APT extends to make it more user-friendly.

You also can install, update, and clean packages with APT and find new packages to install. The packages you can see are dependent on which PPAs you have enabled on your machine.

MANAGING PACKAGES USING APT-GET

You can use the package apt-get command to install and update the available packages to your system. APT uses a local database of containers, tells the system updates if available.

Keeping your database up to date is extremely important, as using out-of-date packages leads to security issues on your machine.

To make your APT database update, you can use the following command:

```
$ sudo apt-get update
```

There are three types of an update to the APT database:

1. **Hit**: It means there has been no change to the package since the last check.

2. **Ign**: It means the package has been ignored because it is so recent that there is no need to check it or because there is a slight error.

3. **Get**: It means a package update is available, and APT will now download the details for any update, but not the update itself.

Once you update your database, you can use APT to update the packages on your system and update applications and the Ubuntu core system to the latest versions available:

$ sudo apt-get upgrade

UPGRADE A SPECIFIC PACKAGE

If you want to upgrade your package rather than the whole system. APT allows you to do using the following command:

$ sudo apt-get upgrade [package-name]

It will then update that specific package. It can be helpful if there is a known bug with a particular package, yet you still want to upgrade others.

DIST-UPGRADE

APT has a slightly different way of upgrading your packages; its tool is known as dist-upgrade. dist-upgrade is used in the same way as the standard upgrade command given below:

$ sudo apt-get dist-upgrade

COMBINING COMMANDS

It is essential to run an update before an upgrade when you use APT, but some may find running various commands frustrating. Thus, you can combine commands in Ubuntu so that one command can execute two functions.

You can carry out an update followed by an upgrade, and you can run this command:

$ sudo apt-get update -y && sudo apt-get upgrade -y

SEARCHING FOR PACKAGES

APT helps find new packages. There are better ways of finding new packages, and the command apt-cache does come into play when you are looking for a specific lib or package.

you can use the following command to search for a package using APT,

$ apt-cache search [search term]

INSTALL AND REMOVE PACKAGES USING APT

Like the previous sudo apt-get update, the install command from APT is you have come across when you install new applications with Ubuntu and APT.

The following command to install a package using APT is:

$ sudo apt-get install [package name]

to remove a package using APT, you run the following command :

If you need to continue to learn about APT, you can have a flick through the APT man pages using the following command:

$ man apt

UBUNTU DESKTOP VS. UBUNTU SERVER

Ubuntu ranks as the most popular Linux operating system. However, Ubuntu differs quite a bit. Within Ubuntu, there are two distinct flavors: a stable release and long-term support iteration.

Ubuntu divides into Ubuntu Cloud, Core, Kylin, Desktop, and Server. Here, you will learn about Ubuntu Server and Ubuntu Desktop differences.

WHAT IS UBUNTU DESKTOP?

It is a free, open-source GUI environment, having a Graphical User Interface (GUI). The distribution relies on its command line known as "terminal". Most commands that utilize the terminal for its execution can now use GUI. Its functionality is also in the other popular desktop inter-faces such as Windows and Mac. However, some functions are accessible to perform in the terminal than a GUI.

The file system architecture is similar to the Android O.S. The Files and directories navigate by utilizing the file manager. The default file explorer can be used as simple, but there are multiple alternatives for download if you want to explore more.

It has a lot more options as compared to other distributions. You can also use the terminal or third-party software for their installation, or it has a panel, a toolbar on the left side of the screen, known as "dash" (means dashboard). The dash contains a home button, customization icons of your favorite programs.

Much functionality comes built-in on the Ubuntu Desktop. Many other applications currently in the online repositories may be down-loaded using the Software Centre. Here is the list of some built-in utili-ties: LibreOffice, Movie Player, Thunderbird, Firefox, Gedit, and Ubuntu One Music Store.

WHAT IS UBUNTU SERVER?

It provides a whole operating system and works with a command-line interface rather than with GUI. After installing Ubuntu Server, you will have a blinking cursor when switching on the Server.

Ubuntu Server is a whole operating system. Ubuntu's Server does not come with a Graphical user interface but a command-line interface. Once you install it, you can turn on your Server and are presented with nothing but a blinking cursor.

It has only the minimal necessities for use, and both Ubuntu Server and Desktop use the same repositories application. The server operating system is designed to be used alone; none of the desktop utilities defined above are preinstalled in the Ubuntu Server.

After setting up Ubuntu Server, you can install software via the com-mand prompt when installing Server. The software packages are DNS server, Mail server, Samba File server, Print server, LAMP server, OpenSSH server, Tomcat Java server, Virtual Machine, etc.

After installing it, you can use the command prompt to install the other necessary software to your Server. After installing Ubuntu Server, you can select a software package to install with your operating system that is par-ticular to the type of service to build.

The available software packages are:

- **DNS server**: It selects the BIND DNS server and its documentation.

- **LAMP server**: It prefers a ready-made Linux/Apache/MySQL/PHP server.

- **Mail server**: It chooses a variety of packages useful for a general-purpose mail server system.

- **OpenSSH server**: It picks packages needed for an OpenSSH server.

- **PostgreSQL database**: It selects client and server packages for the PostgreSQL database.

- **Print server**: It sets up your system to be a print server.

- **Samba File server**: It sets up your system to be a Samba file server, which is especially suitable in networks with both Windows and Linux systems.

- **Tomcat Java server**: It installs Apache Tomcat and needs dependencies.

- **Virtual Machine host**: It includes packages required to run KVM virtual machines.

- **Manually select packages**: It executes aptitude allowing you to choose. individually packages.

WE WILL TALK ABOUT THE DIFFERENCE BETWEEN UBUNTU SERVER AND THE DESKTOP VERSION

The desktop environment is the fundamental difference between Ubuntu Server and the Desktop. Desktop and Server lacks a graphical user interface.

Because most servers are not interacting with the machine, these servers do not use display configuration, mouse, or a keyboard. That is a reason that servers are administered remotely through SSH. Some Linux operating systems offer a Graphical User Interface (GUI), while others do not. As a result, Ubuntu Desktop installs a desktop environment, assuming that your machine has video outputs.

INSTALLATION PROCESS OF UBUNTU SERVER VS. UBUNTU DESKTOP

Ubuntu Server does not have a (GUI) Graphical User Interface. That is why it is installed separately from Ubuntu Desktop. Its Server has a process-driven menu while installing Ubuntu Desktop is similar to installing any other software.

DESKTOP APPLICATIONS OF UBUNTU SERVER VS. UBUNTU

Ubuntu Desktop has some preinstalled general purpose applications such as LibreOffice, an office suite productivity, Firefox Mozilla used as a web browser, and many more.

Ubuntu Server comes with numerous packages based on server requirements. It can thus be used as a web server, email server, samba server, and file server. Bind9 and Apache2 are also two specific packages. Its packages provide client connectivity while maintaining security, whereas Ubuntu Desktop applications are centered on the host machine.

Desktop Performance of Ubuntu Server vs. Ubuntu

There is no need to use a desktop environment to divert resources to server tasks in servers. That's why it has better system performance than the Ubuntu Desktop. If you want to install Ubuntu Desktop and Ubuntu Server are two identical machines with the default specifications, the Server will consistently outperform the Desktop.

UBUNTU SERVER VS. UBUNTU DESKTOP SYSTEM REQUIREMENTS

Now, let talk about the system requirements for setting up Ubuntu Server and Ubuntu Desktop versions. Ubuntu Server requires:

- Desktop Performance
- 512 MB RAM
- 2.5 GB hard drive
- 1 GHz CPU

Whereas Ubuntu Desktop requires:

- 2 GB RAM
- 10 GB of hard drive space
- 2 GHz single-core processor

THE UBUNTU DESKTOP PRELOADED APPLICATIONS

The Ubuntu Desktop has many built-in utilities and more stored in its online repositories. They all are downloadable via the Software Center. Some built-in utilities are:

- **Gedit**: It is a text editor, similar to Notepad and TextEdit

- **Firefox**: It is an Internet browser, similar to Internet Explorer and Safari

- **LibreOffice**: It is an Office Suite, similar to Microsoft Office

- **Empathy**: It is a Chat account manager

- **Thunderbird**: It is an Email Client

- **Ubuntu One Music Store**: It is a music store and browser, similar to iTunes

- Movie Player

- Shotwell Photo Manager

CHAPTER SUMMARY

This chapter examines what Linux is and how the vision of better distribution and O.S. became the phenomenon. It moves through Ubuntu's relationship with Canonical, Ltd. and the Ubuntu Foundation. It finishes with some discussion of the various Ubuntu subprojects and derivatives and defines the pros and cons of using Ubuntu over Windows.

CHAPTER 2

Installation of Ubuntu

IN THIS CHAPTER

> ➤ How to Download

> ➤ Installation

> ➤ Understanding the UI

In the previous chapter, we learned what Linux is and how the vision of better distribution and OS became the phenomenon. It moves through Ubuntu's relationship with Canonical, Ltd. and the Ubuntu Foundation, discussing the various Ubuntu subprojects and derivatives and the pros and cons of using Ubuntu over Windows.

BEFORE YOU BEGIN THE INSTALLATION

Installing a new operating system is a most significant event, and you should make sure that you have thought through what is going to occur. However, Ubuntu runs well on various hardware, and it is valuable to check your hardware components because some bits of hardware do not work well with Ubuntu.

This portion provides some areas for you to investigate and think about; it might save you hours of frustration when something goes wrong, and problems are becoming much less frequent, but they still crop up occasionally.

DOI: 10.1201/9781003311997-2

You can start by researching and documenting your hardware, and the information will prove helpful later on during the installation.

At the absolute, you should know the basics of your system, such as how much RAM you have, what type of mouse, keyboard; knowing the storage capacity, kind of hard drive you have is crucial because it helps you plan how to divide it for Ubuntu and troubleshoot if problems occur. The more information you have, the better prepared you are for any issues.

Again, the things you want to consider should include the amount of installed memory, the size of the hard drive, the type of mouse, the capabilities of the monitor, and the number of installed network interfaces.

CHOOSING YOUR UBUNTU VERSION

People are installing Ubuntu for various purposes on desktops, servers, laptops, and so on using different types of computers like PCs and Macs, 32-bit and 64-bit computers, and so on.

INSTALLATION

To install Ubuntu Desktop from the disk included with this book, you should first test whether your system is compatible by running Ubuntu from the DVD live. Your system must have at least a 2 GHz dual-core processor with 25 GB of hard drive space, 2GiB RAM, and a monitor with a display resolution of at least 1024×768. You also need a DVD drive for the installer media. Internet is not required but is very helpful and also recommended.

When choosing a Linux for beginners, Ubuntu always comes on the top list. We are going to tell you why you should use Ubuntu and also going to show you how to install Ubuntu.

THERE ARE MANY OTHER VARIES WAYS TO INSTALL UBUNTU OR OTHER LINUX

- You can install it inside a VirtualBox in Windows.

- You can use the Bash on Windows feature to install it in Windows.

- You can use dual-boot Ubuntu with Windows so that you can also choose which OS to use at the time the system boots.

- You can replace the Windows system with Ubuntu by wiping it all together from your system.

WHAT DO YOU NEED TO INSTALL UBUNTU

- A USB at least 4 GB in size and with a DVD.

- For downloading Ubuntu, an internet connection.

- Optionally, you should need an external USB disk for making a backup of your important data present on the current system.

IF YOU INSTALL THE DEFAULT UBUNTU GNOME, THE SYSTEM REQUIREMENTS ARE

- A system with a 2 GHz dual-core processor or better

- RAM of 4 GB or more

- A hard disk of at least 25 GB

IS IT STILL UBUNTU?

Some of you might read about Kubuntu, Ubuntu Server Edition, and Xubuntu and wonder how different they are from the regular Ubuntu release. As such, they may vary quite a bit, especially in the user interface look and feel, but the underlying operating system and software install system are the same.

GETTING UBUNTU

It is a free OS. When you get a copy of it, you can give it to as many people as you like. These characteristics of Ubuntu mean that it is simple to get a copy. If you have a high-speed internet connection, you can download the .iso file from www.ubuntu.com/download, and then you should follow the instructions.

You can buy Ubuntu authorized Ubuntu CDs at www.ubuntu.com/download/ubuntu/cds.

When you download an Ubuntu in CD, you download a particular .iso file, the same size as a CD. The file is an "image" of the installation CD, and when you burn the .iso file to the CD-ROM, you must have a complete installation CD all ready to go.

WHAT IS AN IMAGE?

When you read about .iso files, you will often see referred to as CD images. The term image doesn't refer to a visual image such as a photo or picture but an actual digital copy of the contents of a CD.

You want to use a CD-burning application to burn your .iso file to the CD correctly then inside the application, and there should be a menu option called Burn the Disk Image or something similar. The details can be altered according to the program you use to burn the image. You must select the .iso file, insert a blank CD, and after a few minutes out will pop a fresh Ubuntu installation CD.

BURNING A CD

The following are instructions for burning a CD in some popular tools to give you a head start.

In Windows, the following steps are to burn your image Windows:

1. Right-click on the icon on the downloaded .iso image and then select open with > Ubuntu Disc Image Burner.

2. Select a writable CD drive from the drop-down box.

3. Click on Burn.

IN WINDOWS

In the older versions of Windows with ISO Recorder, burn your .iso file with the available ISO Recorder.

Follow these steps to burn your image:

1. Insert an empty CD into your CD driver.

2. Now, locate the .iso file you have downloaded, right-click, and select copy-paste the image to CD.

3. Click to record the process begins and when the image has been written, click Finish to leave ISO Recorder.

IN MACOS

When using macOS way to burn your image, follow these steps:

1. Load the Disk Utility application.

2. Insert a blank CD, choose Images > Burn, and select the .iso file.

In Ubuntu, to burn image using Ubuntu, follow these steps. To burn images using Mac OS X, follow these steps:

1. Insert a blank CD into your system CD writer.

2. In the File Browser menu, right-click on the file you early downloaded and choose to Write to Disk. The write to Disk dialog box will open.

3. In the box, choose your CD writer and speed, and then click on the Write option. The Writing Files to Disk Progress box opens, and File Browser begins writing the disk.

Creating a Bootable USB Stick

To create a bootable USB stick, you should follow these steps for your current operating system.

Use a USB stick only with at least 2 GB of free space.

Follow these steps to create a bootable USB stick using Windows:

1. Download the USB installer and follow these installation instructions.

2. Then, insert your stick into the computer and run the USB installer.

3. Select Desktop Edition from the menu.

4. Now browse and select the Ubuntu .iso image you downloaded.

5. Select the USB drive for installation and click Create.

IN MAC OS X,

The Ubuntu download page recommends to Mac users to install using a CD because the workarounds required to create a bootable USB sticks on OS X are complex.

To create a bootable USB stick using Ubuntu, follow these instructions:

1. Insert your USB stick into the computer.

2. Open the Dash and search for Startup Disk Creator. Click the icon for Startup Disk Creator to run the program.

3. Select your downloaded Ubuntu .iso image. If you downloaded .iso, the image does not automatically appear in the list in Startup Disk Creator; click Other to select it.

In Ubuntu to create your bootable USB stick using Ubuntu, follow these steps

1. Insert your USB stick into the computer.

2. Open the Dash and search for Startup Disk Creator. Click the icon for Startup Disk Creator to run the program.

3. Select your downloaded Ubuntu .iso image. If you downloaded .iso, the image does not automatically appear in the list in Startup Disk Creator; click Other to select it.

4. Select the USB stick in the bottom box.

5. Click Make Startup Disk.

There are two methods of installing Ubuntu in your windows laptops are given below

1. By downloading the .iso file and creating the virtual machine, or

2. By burning CD or DVD with .iso file.

Let's discuss both methods one by one, so first by creating the virtual machine of Ubuntu in VirtualBox.

- First, download the VirtualBox from its official website, https://www.virtualbox.org/wiki/Downloads. It can take a long time to download but install it on your Windows operating system once it gets downloaded.

Name of the Website

- Next, you have to click the download button to get the VirtualBox.

VirtualBox is being actively developed with frequent releases and has an ever growing list of features, supported guest operating systems and platforms it runs on. VirtualBox is a community effort backed by a dedicated company: everyone is encouraged to contribute while Oracle ensures the product always meets professional quality criteria.

Name of the Website

Once you click on this button, .exe of VirtualBox file, new window will open as given below:

VirtualBox binaries

By downloading, you agree to the terms and conditions of the respective license.

If you're looking for the latest VirtualBox 6.0 packages, see VirtualBox 6.0 builds. Please also use version 6.0 if you need to run VMs with software virtualization, as this has been discontinued in 6.1. Version 6.0 will remain supported until July 2020.

If you're looking for the latest VirtualBox 5.2 packages, see VirtualBox 5.2 builds. Please also use version 5.2 if you still need support for 32-bit hosts, as this has been discontinued in 6.0. Version 5.2 will remain supported until July 2020.

VirtualBox 6.1.30 platform packages

- ⇨Windows hosts
- ⇨OS X hosts
- Linux distributions
- ⇨Solaris hosts
- ⇨Solaris 11 IPS hosts

The binaries are released under the terms of the GPL version 2.

See the changelog for what has changed.

You might want to compare the checksums to verify the integrity of downloaded packages. The SHA256 checksums should be favored as the MD5 algorithm must be treated as insecure!

- SHA256 checksums, MD5 checksums

New of the Website

You can see the following links. It is just a .exe file based on various operating systems such as:

– VirtualBox 6.1.30 platform packages

– Windows hosts

– OS X hosts

– Linux distributions

– Solaris hosts

– Solaris 11 IPS hosts

When you click on the links, you will get a .exe file as per your system, whether it is Windows, Linux, macOS, and so on.

• After that, you need to install it just by running the exe file which you have already installed. For steps on how to download and install VirtualBox, follow the link. Windows 10 is available on

Microsoft's official web page. Here you will either have to log in or register for Windows inside a program to gain access to the download. Make sure you download the ISO.

- After clicking on the icon, the window will open.

Virtual Box Installation Step 1

- Click on Next on the button and make everything as is it.

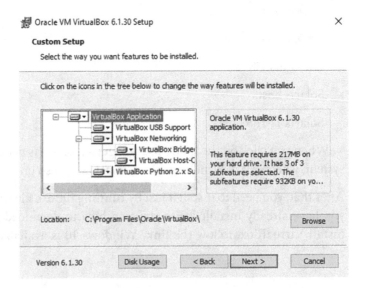

Virtual Box Installation Step 2

The next window will be,

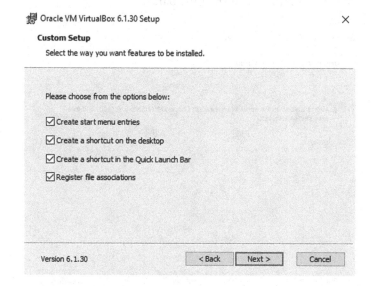

Virtual Box Installation Step 3

- Again you will get popup windows as a custom setup; click on yes.

Virtual Box Installation Step 4

- Then you will get new popup windows with a progress bar. It might take a while to start the bar.

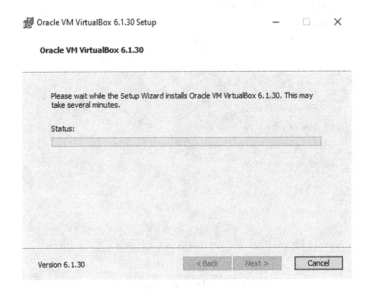

Virtual Box Installation Step 5

- Once your Ubuntu installation is complete, you will see these windows. After this, your VirtualBox installation is completed.

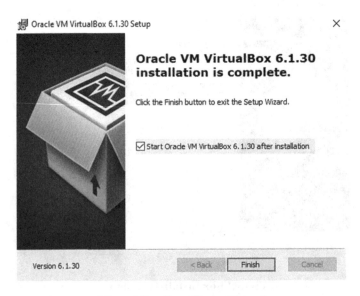

Virtual Box Installation Step 5

VIRTUALBOX

All the above steps are related to the VirtualBox downloading and installation. So now we are going to create the new virtual machine in the VirtualBox. Here are the steps are given below,

- Open VirtualBox and select "new machine". You should be able to do this once you've installed VirtualBox screen.

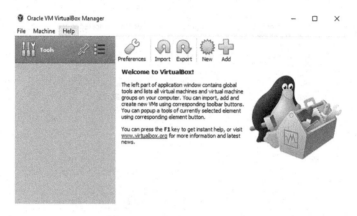

Virtual Box Manager Screen

- Type in "Ubuntu LTS" into the text box. You can type in, or you can choose a different name for the operating system if you prefer. Once this is done, select "Linux" on the first scroll menu, and then select "Ubuntu LTS" from the version box (second scroll box).

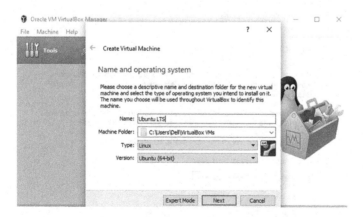

Virtual Box Ubuntu LTS Installation

- Select how much RAM you would like to give the Ubuntu machine. When the Windows wizards asks you how much RAM to give the machine, then giving the default amount of RAM should be fine, but if you have a lesser or limited RAM, then adjusting using the slider is good for you.

Selecting RAM for Ubuntu installation

• When the wizard window asks about a new virtual hard disk, do not select anything. Simply select "Next".

Hard disk recommendation

- Select the disk file type as VDI (VirtualBox Disk Image), then click Next.

Hard disk file type

- Set your disk space for the hard drive. The wizard asks you to set the disk space for your hard drive; you can select a dynamically allocated or a fixed size also may choose either; it is often better to choose a fixed size, as it is usually faster and more stable.

File location and Size

Select disk size 20 gigabytes. It should be selected as a minimum, but the more space, the merrier.

- Then click on the setting of the VirtualBox. The dialog will open then you can see the number of options on the left of the window, such as general system, display, and so on. Just click on the system and change the following setting, like remove the tick in the front of the Floppy and click ok.

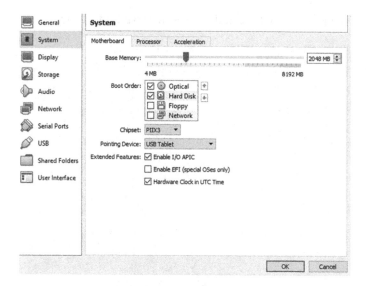

Setting of Floppy disk

- Now move to another option that is storage. Click on the first button and add the.iso file of the Ubuntu that you already download from their official website in it. After adding it click on the Choose button and then ok.

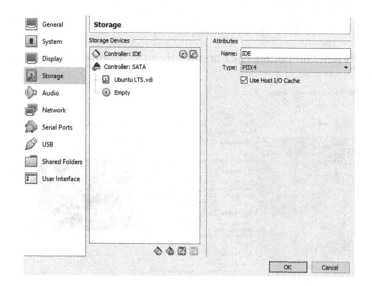

Storage setting in a virtual setting

Then the file will be added to your virtual machine.

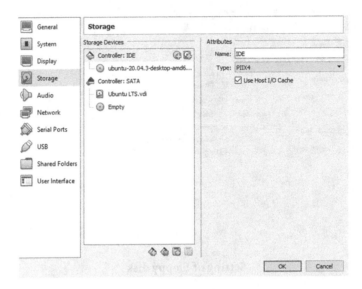

Adding Ubuntu iso file.

Ubuntu has been booted, and now you are ready to use it using a virtual box. The important step is to install Ubuntu on your VirtualBox machine.

Here the steps are as follows,

When you double click on the Ubuntu LTS image is given below,

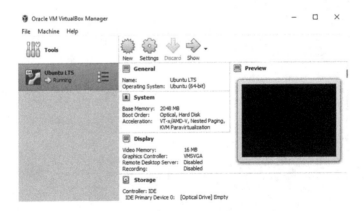

Double click on the Ubuntu LTS image icon

After that, you will get a screen, and that is the point where the checking of all the files in progress for further installation. It might take some time to check all the files.

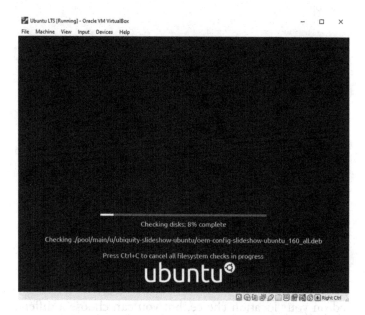

Checking all the files for further installation.

Ubuntu provides a migration assistant to ease your transition to your new OS. If your supported OS is found during installation, and you are presented with a list of accounts that can be migrated. You can choose to migrate anything; you must provide details for the new user to whom the features will be migrated.

The screen you are presented first with when you restart the computer introduces you to the installation program and asks you to select your language.

Whether you want to Try Ubuntu or whether you want to install Ubuntu, Ubuntu supports a vast range of different languages. Pick your preferred language from the given list and click Install Ubuntu to continue installing.

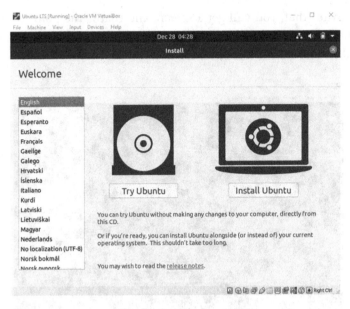

Click on install the Ubuntu.

On the next screen, the installer will suggest a keyboard option based on your location choice, but you can choose a different one. You can also use the box at the bottom of the window to test whether your keyboard layout works and then click on continue.

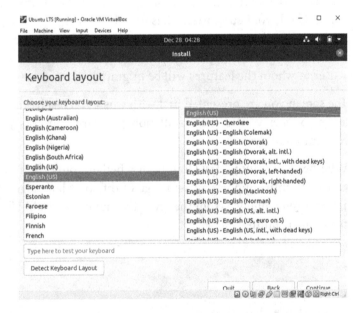

Pick your preferred language for the default keyboard.

Download updates while installing Ubuntu as given below,

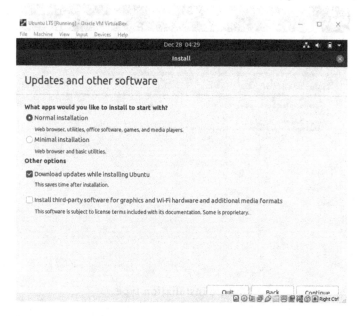

Download update options.PNG

We strongly suggest you select the option to Download Updates While Installing because if you want to include any existing security updates or bug fixes, this option will end your installation with a current up-to-the-minute system. A nice feature is that these updates will be downloaded while installation is in process, parallel to other operations, so it happens with excellent efficiency. You may even choose to install third-party software to enable your system to play specific media files immediately after installation. It also saves your time later, although some users may not want to install closed-source software and will choose not to enable this option. Click Continue after making your selections.

In the next step, you will have installation type using two ways either you can erase your hard disk fully to install Ubuntu in your VirtualBox machine or something else like you give only maximum space to your new Ubuntu system it is totally up to your choice.

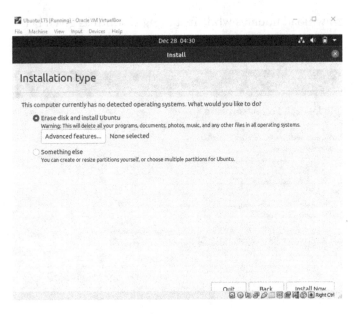

Ubuntu installation type

When you press Continue, you will get another window where you see that you can make changes to your hard disk manually. If not, then just click Continue again.

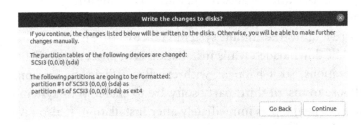

manually change disk size.

At this point, the installation begins. While it goes, you will ask questions to customize your installation appropriately. Tell the installer where in the world you live.

Tell the installer about your location.

The other step is to enter some personal details about you that you can use to create a user account on the computer.

In the first box of your name, enter your full name. The information is used in different system parts to indicate who the user is behind the account.

Enter a computer name in the list box. It is also called a "username," a single word identifying your current machine. It is used on a local network to determine which device is which.

In the second box, the -VirtualBox is automatically suffixed to your name, and then your name's first part is picked as your nickname.

Please enter a password in the following two boxes and then confirm it. The password is used for logging in to your computer with the username you just created.

While choosing a password, follow these simple guidelines.

It would be best if you remember your password. If you need to write it down, keep it somewhere secure.

You should avoid using dictionary words ("real words") such as "name of your dog."

Your password should be longer than six letters and a combination of letters, symbols, and numbers. The longer the password and the more it mixes with uppercase, lowercase letters, numbers, and symbols, the more secure it becomes.

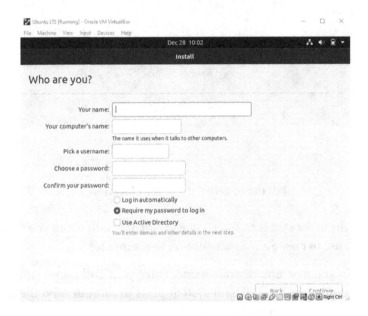

Identification of system

From here, as Ubuntu continues to be installed on your system, you have displayed a figure containing valuable and exciting information about the operating system. You will be asked to restart your computer at the end of the process.

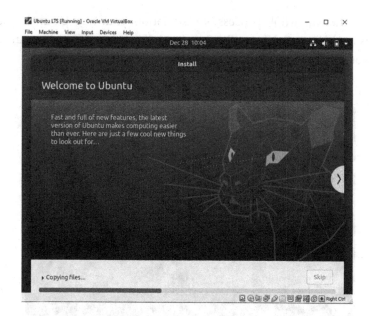

Installation begins.PNG

And your restart will be like,

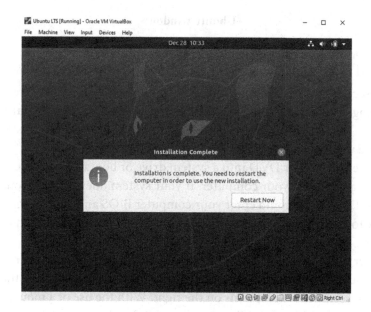

Restart window

After the whole process of installation, your new Ubuntu system is ready in your VirtualBox machine. You can use it just by running your Virtual Box. Ubuntu's first window will look like this.

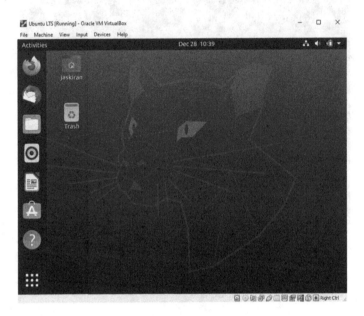

Ubuntu windows

Another method of Booting and Installing Ubuntu by using burned CD/DVD/ USB Stick

This section has instructions for running Ubuntu from the desktop CD burning. You can explore and test Ubuntu without changing your hard drive. If you do not like it, reboot and remove the CD/DVD/USB stick to replace what you already have.

Place your CD or DVD into a system drive or bootable USB stick into a port, and reboot your computer. If your system doesn't boot from the CD or DVD, you should enter your computer BIOS and change the boot order to ensure boot medium. Save your BIOS changes, and then again restart.

After a few moments, the Ubuntu logo with boot screen appears, and then you are presented with a complete list of various languages on the left of the screen with two options on the right. With the use of a mouse, you can select your language. Then you can decide whether you want to try

Ubuntu 12.04, which allows you to try out Ubuntu without making any changes to your computer and install it later.

And if you decide you want to install Ubuntu 12.04 version, which will jump into the installer, select the option, and Ubuntu will begin to boot. The Ubuntu desktop will appear after a minute, and you can use the system straight. The system is running from the CD and will not touch your hard disk with this scenario. Remember that because Ubuntu is running from the CD, it will run slower than if it were installed on your hard disk.

ALLOCATE DRIVE SPACE

To prepare your hard-to-store Ubuntu system, your hard disks are divided into partitions. Each partition has a specific portion of the hard disk.

As an example, you may use the complete hard disk for your Ubuntu system, or you can share the disk so that Windows' and Ubuntu are installed. This scenario is known as dual-booting.

In a dual-booting, your hard disk typically has Windows partitions and Linux partitions, and when it boots, it gives you a menu to select whether to boot Windows or Linux.

In this installer part, you create the partitions for your new system. This can be the tough part of the installation and the most dangerous. If you have existing partitions on the disk, it is highly recommended to back up your essential files.

If you have decided to install the system permanently on your computer's hard disk, there are two ways you can do so:

1. Double-click the Install icon located on the left side of the desktop.

2. Reboot and select Install Ubuntu from the initial menu.

Using this option, an installer walks you through the steps to permanently install your Ubuntu system.

The Ubuntu Desktop: Understanding the UI of Ubuntu Desktop

Getting Started

When you sign into Ubuntu for the first time, you will see the main screen that looks like this.

The Ubuntu default desktop

It is the Ubuntu desktop. While Canonical foundation has added a few charm elements, the interface you see is not exclusive to Ubuntu. It's known as GNOME.

WHAT IS GNOME?

It is a desktop environment with free operating systems that come from the GNU Project, which has provided the other with free software for decades.

Ubuntu uses the kernel to make software communicate with your system, and it uses GNOME to provide you with an easy-to-use on-screen interface. The panel showing the time, the launcher that opens apps, and the overview screen showing all your open windows are all part of GNOME.

When you press Activities in the upper-left corner of the desktop, the screen darkens and displays a new set of controls.

- Open windows are arranged conveniently in the middle of the screen showing you what is running in the background.

- To the right side, you have to switch workspaces. In general, you have various virtual desktops that you can switch between them at any time, giving you more screen space.

- At the top, you will get a search that looks through the applications, files, and apps available for download.

How to Navigate the Ubuntu Desktop

A glance at the desktop shows a panel at the top of the screen and a quick launch bar on the left side.

Ubuntu offers numerous keyboard shortcuts that save our time and effort. To get a list of shortcuts, click Super key + Esc. The key varies with the type of computer:

- The Super key is located next to the left ALT key.

- On a Mac, look for the Command key on the keyboard.

Connect to the Internet

Press the network icon on the top panel. It displays a list of wireless networks. Select any network you wish to connect, then enter its key. If you are associated with the router using an Ethernet cable, you automatically connect to the internet. You can browse the Firefox web.

Keep Ubuntu Up To Date

Ubuntu notifies when updates are available for installation. You can manually set the settings so that the updates work accordingly by running the graphical Software Updater application. If you use the command line, open a terminal window and enter the command below to update the system.

```
$ sudo apt update && sudo apt upgrade -y
```

The GNOME Desktop Interface

It is unlike Windows and macOS, though it has some elements in common. Let's start by looking at the top of the screen.

TOP BAR

The top bar at the top of the screen provides access to the Activities overview, the currently open application's menu, the date and time, and system indicators such as battery life and network connectivity.

Ubuntu windows top bar

Dock

The dock is present on the left side of the screen. It shows actively open apps plus shortcuts to your favorites.

Ubuntu dock.

ACTIVITIES OVERVIEW

The Activities overview is where most of the things happen. It would be best to open the overview by clicking the Activities button on the top bar or dragging your mouse to the top-left corner of the screen.

Activities Overview

APP DRAWER

The app drawer is visible at the bottom of the left side dock. It lists all of the apps installed on your system in a grid of icons when you click on it.

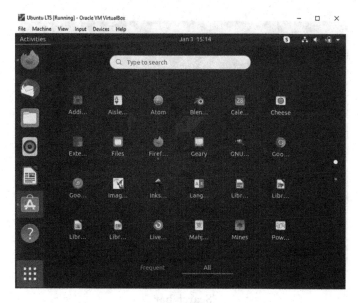

App Drawer

SYSTEM SETTINGS

To configure system settings, search for System Settings or click the settings logo in the power menu which brings up the Settings window, from which you can select entries from the menu at the left and then make adjustments by Finding Programs and Files.

Configuring Power Management in Ubuntu

Select the Power option from the Settings to handle power-saving features in specific situations.

Ubuntu supports suspending, which means your system writes the current state to memory and goes into a low-power mode. Your system will start much faster the next time you use it because it does not need to perform a full boot. Instead of starting every program again from scratch, it brings the system up to its previous state out of memory.

Finding Files, Folder, and Applications

A search bar is visible on the top of the Activities overview. You can open apps, load files, issue commands, and perform numerous other actions by typing into this area.

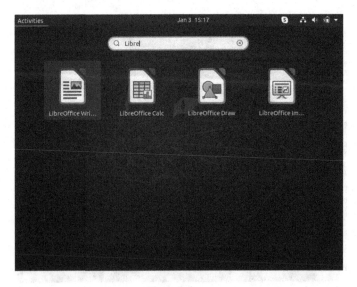

Search bar

Workspaces

These are present on the right corner of the Activities overview, across from the dock—workspaces as numerous desktops that exist virtually on the same computer.

Ubuntu Workspace

Navigating the Top Bar

The item on the top bar is the Activities button. By clicking on it opens the Activities overview.

Next is the application menu, where you can adjust application settings, such as changing the default folder of download for a web browser or changing fonts in a text editor.

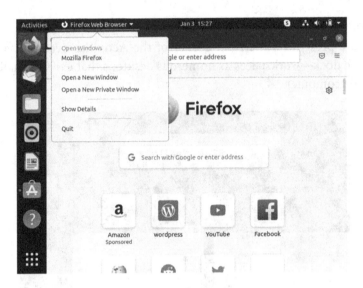

Navigating the Top Bar

The far-right corner holds system indicators. Individual icons show battery life, network connectivity, sound, Bluetooth, and more. However, clicking on any of these indicators opens up a single menu that will let you toggle volume, change your network, restart your computer, and perform other tasks.

Navigating the Dock

A dock having your apps lines the left side of the screen. Unlike other GNOME desktops, the Ubuntu dock is permanently visible yet of whether the Activities overview is open.

(+) Click on an app plus icon to launch the software. If an app opens, that isn't already on the dock, and a new icon will appear.

When you open an app, a red indicator appears next to the icon on the dock. If you open another window, a second dot appears. The indicator maxes out at four windows.

Indicator maxes

Right-clicking an app icon allows you to perform app-specific functions such as opening a new window in Firefox or pausing music in Rhythmbox. It is also how you remove an app stored on the dock or pull up background information about a piece of software.

Menu box after click

Navigating the App Drawer

In the lower-left corner, the app drawer arranges all your installed apps into a grid. The experience is similar to what you encountered on a smartphone or tablet.

You will find the date and time in the middle. Clicking here pulls up a calendar and displays notifications.

Navigating the App Drawer

Navigating the Activities Overview

By clicking on the Activities button, the Activities overview shows all of your open windows.

A search bar is at the top of the overview screen. You can click to perform a search. If you start typing without clicking on the bar, the overview will instantly show search results. You can search for applications, files, folders, and other settings. You can even look for new software in the Ubuntu Software app.

With Ubuntu installed, you are ready to go; it is time to get started using your new operating system. Unlike other operating systems, such as Windows or Mac OS X, Ubuntu includes everything you need to get started: an office suite, media tools, a Web browser, etc.

You may notice many similar things between Ubuntu and other operating systems, such as Microsoft Windows or Mac OS X, because they are all based on the concept of a graphical user interface (GUI). That is, you use your mouse to navigate the move files, desktop, open applications, and perform most other tasks. In short, things are visually oriented. This chapter is designed to help you become familiar with various applications and menus in Ubuntu OS so that anyone can become confident in using the Ubuntu GUI.

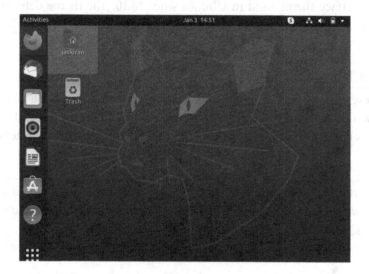

The Ubuntu default desktop.

THE UBUNTU DESKTOP IS UNITY

When reading about Ubuntu, terms like Unity and Ubuntu desktop are used interchangeably.

With the support from Canonical, the Ubuntu community has created the Unity desktop as the next stage in graphical interface evolution if other Linux distributions follow suit or choose to use one of the other existing options.

All GUI-based systems use a desktop environment. It might contain many features, including:

- The organization of the desktop

- How anyone can navigate the desktop

Ubuntu uses Unity as the default desktop environment. The Unity desktop comprises the desktop background, and two bars – a horizontal bar located at the top of the desktop called the menu bar, and a vertically oriented bar at the far left called the Launcher.

Below the main menu at the top of the screen is an image covering the entire desktop. It is the default desktop background or wallpaper, belonging to the default Ubuntu 16.04 theme known as Ambiance or Yaru, the user interface theme used in Ubuntu since 18.10. The theme determines the colors, borders, shadows, size, and shape of individual elements on the screen.

DEVICE ICONS

However, there are no application icons on the desktop. A device icon appears on the desktop when you plug any USB device in the USB port, such as portable music players, other keyring drives, or digital cameras.

THE LAUNCHER

The vertical sidebar of application icons on the left side of the desktop is known as Launcher. It provides easy access to applications, mounted devices, and the bin Trash. To change the Launcher icon's size, go to Session Indicator > System Settings > Appearance under the tab Look.

Ubuntu Launcher.PNG

The Ubuntu Launcher is on the left with a sample of applications.

To find or run an application, you can simply use the Launcher. The Launcher is on the left of the screen. The icon bar shows icon links for applications and indicates which applications are open with a small arrow. If you open more applications than shown in the Launcher, the Launcher will "fold" the application icons at the bottom of the Launcher.

At the bottom of the bar, you will find the dash icon. It shows you your running applications. Click on any icon in the dash to open that application. If it is already running, it will have a small dot below the icon. By clicking the icon will bring up the most lately used window.

By clicking right on the icon displays a menu that allows you to pick a window in a running application or open a new window. You can even click the icon while holding down Ctrl to open a new window.

Other Icons in the Launcher

In extra to the Ubuntu Launcher includes several valuable icons by default. Even so, these icons deserve a quick remark, listed in the order they appear in the Launcher from top to bottom.

- **Home Folder**: It opens your home folder using the file manager, which is described next.

- **Ubuntu Software Center**: It opens your primary software management system for Ubuntu. Workplace Switcher lets you have four different screens for your desktop, with various programs active in each, and switch between them. It is excellent to have many things open at once and run out of space on your screen. For example, you can be using your web browser and email client while talking to others in a chat client on the desktop and working on a document on the second desktop. You can click each virtual desktop to switch to it to access your different applications.

- **Trash**: It is where files you throw away go until you empty the Trash to remove them permanently. Files dragged onto the icon or right-clicked, moved to Trash are destined to be deleted. To delete these files, just right-click the Trash and select Empty Trash.

Start Applications

- Move your mouse cursor to the Activities corner at the top left of the screen to show the Activities overview, where you can find all of your applications.

- There are various ways of opening an application in the Activities overview.

- When you start adding the name of an application, the searching begins instantly.

- You can add applications to the dash yourself if you have applications that you use frequently.

- Click the grid button that has nine dots in the dash. You will see the first page of installed applications. To list all the applications, press the dots at the bottom.

Applications that are presently running will have one or more triangles on the left side of the icon, demonstrating the number of application windows open. Running applications also have a back-lit icon on the Launcher.

A single white triangle indicates the application in the foreground on the right side of its icon.

UBUNTU APPLICATIONS

The GNOME environment, the next step to start using compatible programs and applications. If you recently migrated from another operating system, you might not know what is available and what programs you use.

Below is a listing of essential programs and applications for managing your system, most of which are preinstalled on Ubuntu.

HOW DO I UPDATE MY COMPUTER?

Installing Ubuntu onto your computer, and you need to make sure your system is safe, secure, and up to date by using the Software Updater. The program will regularly install security updates and critical bug fixes for all your software.

How Do I Download Software and Applications?

If you are not sure which software programs are compatible with Ubuntu, look no other than Ubuntu Software, an application that allows downloading, installing, and removing the software without launching an internet browser.

Ubuntu Software is accessible through your launcher as well as the app drawer. Use it to discover free applications, games, fonts, and other tested and validated software to work seamlessly with Ubuntu.

WITH UBUNTU SOFTWARE

- You can search, download, install, and remove software in a single window.

- You can keep track of installation, update, and removal history.

- You can read and write user reviews.

- You can receive software recommendations based on your search and installation history.

How Do I Browse the Web?

Mozilla Firefox is the most popular web browser, and the default comes with the installation of Ubuntu. Firefox is the default web browser in several Linux distributions, and Ubuntu is one. Firefox comes preinstalled in Ubuntu unless you are using it.

Installing Firefox on Ubuntu

It is available in all the Linux distributions out there. It is also preinstalled in most of them. Open the software center and enter Firefox in the search bar. You should see it there and click on the install button.

If you prefer the command prompt, open a terminal and use the following command in Ubuntu and other distributions based on Ubuntu, such as Linux Mint, elementary OS, etc.

```
$ sudo apt install firefox
```

HOW DO I MANAGE MY EMAIL ACCOUNTS?

Thunderbird is the default email app in Ubuntu and a commonly used email on all major operating systems. You can use Thunderbird to consolidate and manage all of your email accounts and contacts in a window without launching a browser.

Mozilla Thunderbird Email Application

Thunderbird is a free and open-source email, newsfeed, chat that's easy to set up and customize. The core principles of Thunderbird are the same as the use of an open standard. We want users to have freedom and choose how they communicate.

Set Up Your Existing Email Address	⊗

Set Up Your Existing Email Address
Use your current email address

Your name:	Your full name	ⓘ
Email address:	Your email address	ⓘ
	Get a new email address...	
Password:	Password	⬤
	☑ Remember password	

Mozilla Thunderbird email application

You can install snap from the command line:

$ sudo apt update
$ sudo apt install snapd

Another method to install Thunderbird use the following command:

sudo snap install thunderbird

How Do I Listen to Music?

Rhythmbox is the default application for Ubuntu. You can use it to play albums, organize audio files, create playlists, listen to podcasts, and get other online media.

Below is the command of installing Rhythmbox in your Ubuntu system.

$ sudo apt install Rhythmbox

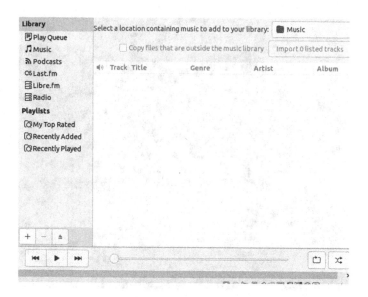

Rhytmbox Application

It is easy-to-use music playing and management program that supports a wide range of audio formats (including mp3 and ogg). Initially inspired by Apple's iTunes, the current version also supports Internet Radio, iPod integration and generic portable audio player support, Audio CD burning, Audio CD playback, music sharing, and podcasts.

HOW DO I ORGANIZE MY PHOTOS?

Ubuntu has several packages for managing photos and viewing and editing images. Shotwell Photo Manager Application is the default photo application in Ubuntu. You can use Shotwell to import your photos, organize them, and view them on your computer. Below is the command of installing Shotwell in your Ubuntu system.

    $ sudo apt install Shotwell

Shotwell Application

It is a digital photo organizer designed for the GNOME desktop environment. It allows importing photos, pictures, and videos from a disk or camera and organizing them in various collections. The viewer shows in full-window or fullscreen mode and presents as galleries or slideshows. The editor can rotate, flip, crop, and tag the photos, adjust the colors and remove the red-eye, and perform various things in a single go.

Eye of GNOME, an essential image viewer, allows you to view photos in a folder, zoom in and out, and rotate images.

HOW DO I WATCH VIDEOS?

Ubuntu comes with the Totem Movie Player that can automatically load videos saved to your hard drive, playing them back in a minimalist interface. If the totem is not available in your system, you can easily download it using the command line. Below is the command of installing the Totem Player in your Ubuntu system.

$ sudo apt install totem

Here is the result of running the above command,

```
user@user-VirtualBox:~$ sudo apt install totem
[sudo] password for user:
```

```
Reading package lists. Done
Building dependency tree
Reading state information... Done
totem is has the newest version (3.34.1-2ubuntu2).
totem set to manually installed.
The following packages are automatically installed
and are no longer required:
  linux-headers-5.11.0-27-generic
  linux-hwe-5.11-headers-5.11.0-27
  linux-image-5.11.0-27-generic
  linux-modules-5.11.0-27-generic
  linux-modules-extra-5.11.0-27-generic
Use 'sudo apt autoremove' to remove them.
0 upgraded, 0 new installation, 0 to remove, and 0
not upgraded.
```

Features of Totem Player:

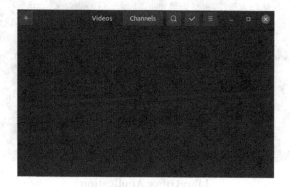

Totem Player Window

- It is a simple featureful media player for GNOME, which can read many file formats.

- It features.

- It supports Shoutcast, m3u, ASX, SMIL, and ra playlists.

- It supports DVD (with menus), VCD, and Digital CD (with CDDB) playback.

- It supports TV-Out configuration with optional resolution switching.

- 4.0, 5.0, 5.1, and stereo audio output.

- Also support fullscreen mode with Xinerama, dual-head, and RandR support.

- Aspect ratio toggling, scaling based on the video's original size.

- Having full keyboard control.

- It is having a simple playlist with repeat mode and saving feature.

How Do I Create Documents like Spreadsheets, Presentations?

LibreOffice is the default office in Ubuntu. It provides the same functionality as MS Word, MS Excel, and MS PowerPoint, where LibreOffice is free and open-source software.

LibreOffice Application

OTHER SOFTWARE PACKAGES

There are widely used packages that you can probably want to use. For example:

- **Steam**: Steam is a platform for gaming, video streaming, and social networking. Install Synaptic and search for it or the apt-get tutorial, and install Steam via apt-get. The package requires a 250 MB update.

- **Minecraft**: It is a popular video game. You can now install Minecraft using the commands of Ubuntu.

- **Wine and Lutris**: It is not an emulator. If you want to play Windows games on Ubuntu, you will need Wine. Lutris is a game organizer and installer who gets games run with Wine.

- **NVIDIA Drivers**: These are graphics drivers that work differently on Linux. If you have a card from NVIDIA, you need the latest drivers. There's a PPA repository to help you with what you need for graphics cards.

- **Spotify**: It is used for streaming music on Ubuntu. You are free to stream from Spotify in a browser with one of the media players that support it. You have the option to install the Spotify client on Ubuntu.

- **Skype**: Microsoft now owns it, so it's understandable if you thought it wouldn't work with Linux. But you can install Skype on Linux.

- **Dropbox**: You can install Dropbox in Ubuntu that is an online storage cloud platform and which you can use as an online backup and for sharing files among colleagues or friends.

UBUNTU COMMUNITIES

Ubuntu Communities, in short LoCos, are groups of users and enthusiasts working together to advocate, promote, translate, develop, and improve Ubuntu. If you're a new Ubuntu user, LoCo can provide advice and technical support.

To find an Ubuntu Local Community, please visit the LoCo Team Directory or contact your nearest LoCo to attend a support event in your city.

Joining LoCo will also provide you with lots of opportunities to get involved and learn new skills. Volunteering contributions can take many forms, and you don't need to be a programmer to help make Ubuntu better. There are many ways to get involved:

1. You can provide advice and technical support to other users.

2. You can write and package new software.

3. You can fix bugs in existing software.

4. You can design graphics, backgrounds, or themes.

5. You can write official and community documentation.

6. You can donate time to promote and advocate Ubuntu.

CHAPTER 3

Desktop Environment

IN THIS CHAPTER

- ➤ Introduction
- ➤ Different desktop environments
- ➤ GNOME
- ➤ Ubuntu MATE
- ➤ KDE
- ➤ Unity and more

In the previous chapter, we have covered the basic installation of Ubuntu using various methods with deep knowledge of the user interface of Ubuntu for beginners to understand its GUI.

INTRODUCTION

It is a collection of software running an operating system that makes up the desktop graphical user interface (GUI). It includes everything from how the windows look and feel to the design of the icons, files, folders, and even mouse pointers. A desktop environment also tells what file manager to use, the default text editor, image viewer, wallpapers, and the interface to log in and out of the local system.

The desktop environment on Microsoft Windows and macOS X is part of the operating system itself. In operating systems such as Linux, the

DOI: 10.1201/9781003311997-3

desktop environment is a modular component that can be changed and reconfigured more easily.

One commonly used term in desktop Linux is desktop environment (DE). You should understand this frequently used term if you are new to Linux.

WHAT IS DESKTOP ENVIRONMENT IN LINUX?

A desktop environment is a set of components that provide standard GUI elements such as icons, toolbars, wallpapers, and desktop widgets. You can use Linux graphically using your mouse and keyboard as you do in other operating systems like Windows and macOS say thanks to the Linux desktop environment.

There are several desktop environments, and these DEs determine what your Linux system looks like and how you interact with it.

Most desktop environments have a group of integrated applications and utilities to get a uniform feel while using the OS. So, you get a file explorer, desktop search, the menu of applications, wallpaper and screensaver utilities, text editors, and more.

Without a desktop environment, your Linux system will have a terminal-like utility, and you will have to interact with it using commands only.

The option varies from system to system, and it changes your whole desktop environment, which might seem otherworldly.

- The desktop environment is what you can call "the graphics shell," enabling the user to interact with the core operating system with their mouse and keyboard.

- It begins with the core Linux operating system and everything you should know from your interactions through the terminal. Working with a Linux system is by typing commands and reading their output.

- X Windows is located on top of the core Linux operating system. It gives the capability to display windows and buttons and enables Linux to understand where you point your mouse or directs forward what you are typing on your keyboard to the specific window.

- It combines a window manager with a group of applications with its toolkit or tested extensively to ensure they "play nice" with it.

- The "toolkit" is a collection of elements, libraries, and other pieces of ready-to-use code.

- Apps made with GTK will be desktop-based, like GNOME and Xfce and with Qt look their best on KDE's Plasma desktop.

Linux Desktop Environment

The primary purpose of distribution is to make utilization of the capabilities of OS. It needs an interface that acts as a bridge for quickly understanding and processing user requirements by the kernel.

Desktop environment precisely does that. It is a graphical interface that presents the bare kernel in a simplified way. Thus, a desktop environment offers all the basic functionalities of a kernel to the user in an elegant and presentable manner.

The components that make up a desktop environment include a file manager that displays all the files and folders in the system in a structured format, window manager, image viewer, video and audio player, calculator, browser, display manager, and all other applications software and utilities you can think of in an operating system.

DIFFERENT DESKTOP ENVIRONMENTS IN LINUX

Some of the desktop environments, such as GNOME, focus on a trendy look and user experience, while desktops like Xfce concentrate more on using fewer computing resources than fancy graphics.

Some of the popular desktop environments are:

- **GNOME**: It uses plenty of system resources but gives you a modern, polished system.

- **Xfce**: It is a vintage look but light on resources.

- **KDE**: It is a highly customizable desktop with moderate usage of system resources.

- **LXDE**: It is entirely focused on using as few resources as possible.

- **Budgie**: It has a modern look and moderates on system resources.

LINUX DISTRIBUTIONS AND THEIR DE VARIANTS

The same desktop environment can be available on several Linux distributions, and a Linux distribution may offer several desktop environments.

For example, Fedora and Ubuntu both use GNOME Desktop by default. But both Fedora and Ubuntu offer other desktop environments.

The beauty and flexibility of Linux are that you can install a desktop environment on any Linux distribution by yourself. But most Linux distributions save you this trouble and offer ready-to-install ISO images for different desktop environments.

For example, Manjaro Linux uses Xfce by default, but you can also download the ISO of GNOME version if you prefer using GNOME with Manjaro.

There are various Linux desktop environments; one example is as follows.

- **GNOME3 Desktop:** GNOME 3 is the default desktop environment. The next version of the GNOME Desktop introduces a new user interface and substantial feature improvements over the last GNOME 2 Desktop dispatched with Red Hat Enterprise Linux 5 and 6.

It is a complete user interface designed to stay out of your way, minimize distractions, and help you get things done. You will see a simple desktop on the top bar when you first log in.

The top bar gives access to your windows and applications, calendar, system properties like sound, power, and networking. In the menu in the top bar, you can change the volume, screen brightness, change your Wi-Fi connection details, check battery status, log out from the system or switch users, and turn off your system.

GNOME 3 provides you with a focused working environment that encourages productivity. A robust search feature lets you access all your work from one place. For instance, you can turn off notifications when you need to concentrate on the task. It is built on many powerful components:

- GNOME Shell
- GNOME Classic
- GNOME Settings
- GVFS
- GTK+

There are various powerful components of GNOME 3. Let's discuss them one by one.

GNOME Classic

It combines old and new; it keeps the familiar look and feel of GNOME 2 but adds the powerful new features and 3-D capabilities of GNOME Shell. GNOME Classic is the default GNOME session and Shell mode in Red Hat Enterprise Linux 7.

GSettings

It is a storage system configuration that replaces GConf found in older GNOME versions.

GVFS

It provides complete virtual file system infrastructure and handles storage in the GNOME Desktop in general. Through GVFS, GNOME 3 integrates well with online document-storage services, calendars, and contact lists, so that your data can access from the same place.

GTK+

It is a multi-platform toolkit for creating graphical user interfaces. It provides a highly usable feature-rich API where GNOME 3 can change the look of an application or give the smooth appearance of graphics. In extra, GTK+ contains several features such as object-oriented programming support (GObject Support), comprehensive support of international character sets and text layouts (such as Pango), or a group of accessibility interfaces (ATK).

What Is a GNOME Shell?

It is the user interface of the GNOME Desktop, the crucial technology of GNOME 3. It provides essential user interface functions such as switching windows, launching applications, or displaying notifications.

It also introduces innovative user interface concepts to provide a quality user experience, including hardware acceleration with modern graphics hardware.

Some of the effective components of the GNOME Shell user interface include:

1. The top bar

2. The system menu

3. The Activities Overview

4. The message tray

Have a look at the following components:

- **The top bar:** The horizontal bar provides access to some of the essential functions of GNOME Shell, such as the Activities Overview, clock and calendar, status icons, and the system menu at the top left corner of the Screen.

- **The system menu:** It is in the top-right corner. You can update some of your settings from this menu, find information about your Wi-Fi connection, switch users, log out, and turn off your computer.

- **The Activities Overview:** These windows and applications views let users run applications and windows and switch between them.

- **Search:** The search at the top allows for searching various items available on the desktop, including applications, documents, files, and configuration tools.

- **Dash:** The bar on the left side in the vertical direction is called Dash and contains a list of favorite and running applications.

- **Workspace:** The workspace list is visible on the right side and allows the user to switch between multiple workspaces or move applications and windows from one workspace to another.

- **The message tray:** It is a horizontal bar near the bottom of the screen and shows when the user presses Super + M and provides access to pending notifications.

COMPONENTS SPECIFIC TO GNOME CLASSIC

It is the default GNOME Shell mode in Linux 7. It can change some elements of GNOME Shell behavior and the GNOME Shell appearance includes the bottom bar with the window list, the Applications and Places menus on the top bar.

What is GNOME Classic?

It is a GNOME Shell feature and mode for users who prefer a more simple desktop experience. While GNOME Classic is based on GNOME 3 technologies, it provides several changes to the user interface:

- **The Applications menu:** It is displayed at the top-left of the screen and gives the user access to applications organized into categories. The user can open the Activities Overview from that menu.

- **The Places menu:** It is displayed next to the Applications menu on the top bar and gives the user quick access to essential folders, for example, Downloads or Pictures.

- **The taskbar:** It is shown at the bottom of the screen and features:

  1. A window list

  2. A notification icon is shown next to the window list

  3. An identifier for the current workspace and the total number of available workspaces is displayed next to the notification icon

  The workspaces available to the user in GNOME Classic are, by default, set to three.

  1. Minimize and maximize buttons

  2. A traditional Super + Tab window switcher

  3. The system menu

  Have a look at these workspaces briefly.

- **Minimize and maximize buttons:** Window title bars feature the minimize and maximize buttons that quickly reduce the windows to the window list or maximize them on the desktop.

- **A Super + Tab window switcher:** In windows in the Super + Tab window, switchers are not grouped by application.

- **The system menu:** It is in the top-right corner. You can update settings from this menu, find information about your Wi-Fi connection, switch users, log out, and turn off your computer.

GNOME Shell Extensions

This section introduces the system-wide configuration of GNOME Shell Extensions. You will learn how to view the extensions, enable them, lock a list of allowed extensions, or set up several extensions as mandatory for the system's users.

You are using dconf when you are configuring GNOME Shell Extensions, setting the following two GSettings keys:

1. org.gnome.shell.enabled-extensions

2. org.gnome.shell.development-tools

What Are GNOME Shell Extensions?

It customizes the default Shell interface and its components, such as window management and application launching.

A unique identifier, the UUID, identifies each GNOME Shell extension. The UUID is also used for the directory's name where an extension is installed. You can either install the extension per user in ~/.local/share/gnome-shell/extensions/uuid, or machine-wide in /usr/share/gnome-shell/extensions/uuid.

The UUID identifier is globally unique. Remember, that when choosing it, the UUID must maintain the following properties to prevent specific attacks:

1. It must not contain Unicode characters.

2. It must not have gnome.org at the end.

3. It must have alphanumerical characters, the period (.), the at symbol (@), and the underscore (_).

The GNOME Classic Extensions

GNOME Classic has a set of GNOME Shell Extensions. These extensions are installed as dependencies of the gnome-classic-session package, which provides components required to run the Classic session. The GNOME Classic extensions default on Linux 7, and GNOME Classic is the Linux 7 desktop user interface.

1. AlternateTab (alternate-tab@gnome-shell-extensions.gcampax.github.com)

2. Applications menu (apps-menu@gnome-shell-extensions.gcampax.github.com)

3. Launch new instance (launch-new-instance@gnome-shell-extensions.gcampax.github.com)

4. Places Status Indicator (places-menu@gnome-shell-extensions.gcampax.github.com)

5. Window List (window-list@gnome-shell-extensions.gcampax.github
   .com)

Components of GNOME include:

- **Metacity**: It is a default window manager.

- **Nautilus**: It is a default file manager.

- **gedit**: It is a default text editor.

- **Eye of GNOME**: It is a default image viewer.

- **GNOME Videos**: It is a default video player.

- **Epiphany**: It is a web browser.

FEATURES OF GNOME 3 DESKTOP ENVIRONMENT

In this section, we look at the new features of the GNOME 3 Desktop
Environment and updates that will change your desktop experience in the
coming days.

You cannot just install/upgrade to GNOME 3 in your standard Linux
distributions right now. The Ubuntu 20.04 LTS version will not get the
GNOME 3.38 update at the moment.

If you want to experience all the latest GNOME features, you have to
wait for more days for it to be packaged and sent to your desktop update
by distributions.

GNOME3 or later was in the development phase for the last couple of
months, and we already featured the changes here. Now, we have the complete feature set to explore what's new in GNOME 3 or later.

- **New Welcome Tour Guide App:** An official welcome app GNOME
  Tour guide appears at the first login after the initial setup.

  With GNOME 3, the Tour app is now revamped, highlighting and
  guiding first-time users to the main functionality of the GNOME
  Desktop.

- **GNOME Web:** GNOME app has received several improvements. If
  you use web browser Chrome but want to shift to GNOME Web, it
  will import bookmarks and passwords from Google Chrome.

For a better browsing experience and privacy, it has enabled Intelligent Tracking Prevention by default and allows you to block websites from storing local data in your browser.

- **Core GNOME Apps Improvements:** GNOME 3.38 has also touched upon several other official GNOME applications along with Tour and Web. For instance, it has redesigned the Screenshot, Sound Recorder, and dialog in the Clocks app.

  Also, its maps can display labels in the satellite view, adapt the user interface for mobile phones, and you can also switch Maps to night mode.

- **Games Collection:** GNOME games collection provides several video games, and then you will be amused to know that games support Nintendo 64 games as well.

  It also lets you organize games into groups for better usability and easy access. Overall, games have received enough performance improvements to become more stable.

- **Different Refresh Rates for Each Monitor:** If you use one or more monitors and want a different refresh rate for each one, it's possible in GNOME 3.38. With the recent improvements to mutter window manager, GNOME Shell lets you have two or more monitors running at different refresh rates.

- **Restart Directly from System Menu:** If you have used the last GMOME 3.36, you may find it annoying to restart the system as you have to click the first "Power Off" button on the System menu and then "Restart".

  Therefore, with GNOME 3.38, you will notice a separate "Restart" button alongside "Power Off" in the System menu.

  Wi-Fi is a technology that lets you share your internet connection with other devices wirelessly. Thus, if you want to turn your Linux system, including GNOME Desktop, into a portable Wi-Fi hotspot, you can directly share QR codes with other devices such as laptops, tablets, and mobile.

- **Custom Application Grid:** It is one of the significant changes to GNOME 3.38. You can move apps to and from by dragging your application icons and creating folders into the application grid.

The icons can scale down for lower screen resolution with better grid customization. Also, GNOME has removed the "Frequent Apps" tab to add support for custom positions that means you can organize and rearrange your apps the way you want.

- **GNOME OS:** It is designed especially for developers involved in the development and testing of GNOME.

  With the recent GNOME apps, which manage virtual machines and remote desktop connections, you can now run GNOME OS images. Hence, if you want to test GNOME 3.38 desktop, images are available to download and install.

- **A Brand New Onscreen Keyboard:** If you own a touch-screen device, you are going to appreciate the new onscreen keyboard in GNOME 3.28.

  The new onscreen keyboard is easier to use. It automatically appears onscreen when you click inside a text area. OSK positions so that the text area is visible while typing.

- **Better Photos:** You will already know about many of the improvements to Photos if you used this site.

  The GNOME Photos can import photos from SD cards and USB drives. Although small, when you connect any device with compatible files, this feature helps speed up adding pictures to your collection.

Further improvements to the GNOME Photos app enable it for the following:

- It can edit shadows and highlights.
- It can change crop orientation.
- It supports zoom gestures.
- It has the option to set the edited photo as wallpaper.
- It completes support for EXIF rotation.

GNOME Photos is becoming one of the real stand-out apps in the GNOME lineup.

- **Flatpak Improvements:** It is becoming the new standard for Linux app distribution, and the fledgling packaging format gets a big boost. It has GTK+ theme handling, language configuration support, and an improved CLI and improved Support for USB, Bluetooth and Thunderbolt Devices. GNOME 3 or later gains support for Thunderbolt 3 devices.

GNOME's Thunderbolt handling includes security checks on connected devices to prevent data theft, showing notifications on connection and statuses, and adding a small "lighteninbolt" icon in the top bar when a compatible Thunderbolt 3 device is attached. You can now keep an eye on the power level of PlayStation controllers.

KDE

What Is KDE in Linux Operating System?

KDE stands for K Desktop Environment is a desktop working platform with a graphical user interface released of an open-source package for Linux-based operating systems as you can think of KDE as a GUI for Linux OS. When KDE was first released, it was named Kool desktop environment, abbreviated as K desktop. The KDE is equipped with everything users typically need, including file, window, help, and system configuration tools.

KDE has proved Linux users to make its use as easy as they use windows. It provides Linux users a graphical interface to choose their customized desktop environment. You can select your graphical interface among various available GUI interfaces with their look.

You can imagine Linux without KDE and GNOME, just like DOS in windows. KDE and GNOME are similar to Windows, except they are related to Linux through x server rather than an operating system. When you install Linux, you have a choice to choose your desktop environment from two or three different desktop environments like KDE and GNOME. Another popular environment, same as KDE, is GNOME. Both come with a combination of features with other distributions. KDE comes with a variety of features.

WHY KDE PLASMA DESKTOP IS SO POPULAR

There are several environments available for Linux. But popular are GNOME, Xfce, Cinnamon, MATE, Unity, and our beloved KDE Plasma. It guides highlights some of the reasons KDE outshines many of these desktop environments.

The following are reasons to use KDE desktop environment:

- **Appearance:** It has been the choice for users looking for a pleasing desktop experience. It is one of the best-looking desktop environments. However the notion of beauty may be different, we are sure that you will agree with us on this matter. The Plasma desktop offers a modern and elegant visible experience thanks to this excellent color choice and delightful animations.

  The shadows make the application widgets look natural, and well-designed icons treat the eyes. It designs all aspects of its appearance with extreme care. So, the widgets, fonts, and mouse pointers are visible pleasing. Moreover, these elements mix well with other GUI components and thus result in a dramatic desktop.

- **Free and open source:** The KDE environment is free and open source. So, it ensures the users get the most beautiful desktop experience without paying anything. This is a big plus for this environment since they can feel what they are getting into, and if they do not like it, they can switch to another environment without facing any loss.

  The open-source code base is available for anyone to analyze. Thus, the seasoned users get the opportunity to play around with the environment and make customizations as they want. This is good for a lot of users. So overall, it allows users to try it freely and determine whether it suits their taste or not without any catches.

- **Ease of use:** Instead of packing a lot of components, KDE Linux systems are straightforward to use. It tries hard to be as user-friendly as possible and provides a good experience to even the newest users. The easy-to-use application widgets and menus make sure uninterrupted workflow. Also, the Krunner app launcher is the best Linux application launchers you can get. You can search files, web pages, toggle between windows, and many more effortlessly.

- **Konsole:** It is the default terminal that ships with the KDE desktop. It is one of the famous Linux terminal emulators suitable for new and advanced users. Its features include the support for split view, ssh bookmarking, otification alerts, true color fonts, profile customization, dolphin integration, n font ligature, and many more. Hence, users can embed Konsole directly into their desktop without displacing existing windows.

Since Konsole provides many features and is not the best terminal in terms of memory usage, it's doubtful to throttle systems with modest resources. Overall the Konsole is an excellent choice for performing everyday tasks and advanced scenarios. If you want the Linux terminal to be as flexible as possible, you will love Konsole.

- **App widgets:** App widgets are an essential part of the KDE user experience. First of all, users can choose from 200 plus widgets. You can also find widgets for almost anything in the KDE world, from small utilities to workflow management. They make displaying system information like networking, weather, CPU usage, and downloading progress directly to the desktop.

- **KDE applications:** The KDE Plasma desktop comes with a handy set of applications. Whether Linux is proficient, the default KDE apps are more than adept for daily tasks. Apart from Krunner and Konsole, other special KDE default applications include the:

  - Dolphin file manager

  - Falkon web browser

  - Konversation IRC client

  - Gwenview image viewer

  It includes a lot of applications for development, education, and a large number of games. In addition, many KDE-powered tools have gained popularity due to their elegant interfaces and competitive feature set. The video editor utility Kdenlive and the digital painting application Krita are great examples. So, you can ensure having all the essential tools if you choose KDE as your desktop environment.

- **Performance:** The ecosystem of KDE is vast and often requires more extensive libraries. The performance is good. The performance has increased dramatically in Plasma 5 and got a smooth, seamless experience that is both flexible and highly customizable. The UX is free from bugs. If you want a good desktop environment without compromising performance, then KDE will be an excellent choice. However, it is not good for low-end CPUs.

- **Customization:** You can personalize all major Linux distributions. KDE has taken them to another level. From widgets to animations, buttons to pointers, docks to panels, you can change nearly every part of KDE as per your taste. Unlike other desktop interfaces, KDE does not restrict customization for a few GUI components.

- **Power usage:** Power consumption has become more critical than ever, especially for portable devices like laptops and notebooks. IDE is not extremely power-hungry in most cases. It also comes with excellent battery management capabilities; ensuring users get the possible screen time out of their devices. However, that power usage depends heavily on your desktop configuration.

- **Multiple desktops:** It provides multiple desktop functionality for users who do many things simultaneously and allows users to group apps or windows based on their usage and place them on different desktops. Seamless switching between several desktops is ensured using the Krunner utility. Overall, multiple desktops make app organizations more accessible and more flexible. However, we highly suggest users invest in various monitors as they help to keep the windows visible all the time.

- **Flexibility:** It is one of the most flexible desktop environments for both new and experienced users. Users can also change how Plasma looks and dictate how the environment works. It is straightforward to manage the connectivity options for Bluetooth and networking. Everyday tasks like power management, brightness adjustment, and external device configuration are also quite simple.

- **Extensions:** It is the way of trying out more functionality in your desktop environment. KDE offers excellent support for expendability through extensions but installing and using extensions are much easier in KDE than GNOME. You can download the needed add-ons directly through the app store, whereas GNOME requires to go to the GNOME extension website and install the add-ons from there.

- **KDE store:** Its store is the official application store for all things related to KDE. You can find the needed to customize your desktop here, such as utilities, themes, icons, and wallpapers. The store makes it easy to install new extensions for workflow enhancement. Users can choose from thousands plus components directly from their system, unlike another desktop like GNOME. Overall, KDE Store is an excellent feature of customizing the desktop quickly.

The MATE is the desktop environment of GNOME 2. It provides an intuitive and pleasing desktop environment using traditional metaphors for Linux and other UNIX-like operating systems.

UBUNTU MATE

The MATE is the desktop environment of GNOME 2. It provides an intuitive and pleasing desktop environment using traditional metaphors for Linux and other UNIX-like operating systems.

It is under active development to support new technologies while preserving a traditional desktop experience.

Ubuntu MATE is an operating system the core software that runs your computer, similar to Microsoft Windows, Apple OS X, and Google Chrome OS. Suppose you are new to Ubuntu MATE or only casually acquainted with Linux-based distributions. In that case, it can be challenging to understand how an operating system compares with other systems that you may already be familiar. Hopefully, this section will help demystify Ubuntu MATE for newcomers and reference all users.

The MATE Desktop is a Desktop Environment that implements the desktop made of a set of programs running on top of an operating system, which share a standard graphical user interface. Desktop GUIs help users access and edit files easily. The MATE Desktop is such implementation of a desktop environment. It includes a file manager who can connect you to your local and networked files, archive manager, image viewer, a text editor, calculator, document viewer, system monitor, and terminal—all of our highly customizable and managed via a control center. You can get complete documentation for the MATE Desktop Environment and its applications from its user guide. It provides an intuitive and pleasing desktop environment using traditional metaphors, which means if you have used Microsoft Windows or Apple Mac OS previously, it will feel very familiar. The MATE Desktop has a rich history and continues the GNOME2 desktop, which was the default desktop environment on many Linux and UNIX operating systems for over a decade. This means that MATE Desktop is tried, tested, and very reliable. The name "MATE" is pronounced Ma-Tay. It comes from the yerba maté plant, native to South America.

OBJECTIVES

Ubuntu MATE has multiple objectives and goals:

- It is accessible to all, nonetheless of language and physical ability.

- It increases both Ubuntu and MATE Desktop user adoption.

- This Ubuntu alternative is for computers that are not powerful enough to run a composited desktop.

- Ubuntu platform is for remote workstation solutions like LTSP and X2Go.

- It recreates the halcyon days of Ubuntu for users who prefer a traditional desktop metaphor.

- It uses themes and artwork similar to Ubuntu to familiarize Ubuntu MATE immediately.

- When possible, it contributes to Debian so that both the Debian and Ubuntu communities benefit.

- Its software selection will favor functionality and stability over lightness and whimsy.

MODERN AND FULL-FEATURED

Ubuntu MATE is a modern operating system with an attractive, easy-to-understand user interface. Its update manager keeps the operating system itself and all of its installed applications updated to the current release. Today, the system is more secure and nicely supported than operating systems pre-installed on most home computer hardware.

PRE-CONFIGURED YET FLEXIBLE

Ubuntu MATE provides you the freedom to run a complete, fully featured operating system, pre-configured with most of the applications you need for your daily computing or to change anything about the way it looks, works, or the applications runs to suit your taste.

BUILT-IN SECURITY

It is designed to keep security in mind. Like other operating systems that update only once a month, it receives updates continuously. The updates include security patches for MATE and all of its components. Security updates for all installed applications are also provided on the same plan. It ensures that you have the latest protection for all of your computer's software as soon as it's available.

OPEN SOURCE

Open-source software can be freely used, changed, and shared by anyone. Linux, Ubuntu, and MATE Desktop all have open source and are free.

Although you will find some versions of Linux for purchase, the majority are provided free of charge, like Ubuntu MATE. Open-source software allows anyone to give it away for free. For example, the license gives the user community the freedom to use Linux for any purpose, distribute, modify, redistribute, or sell the operating system.

If you modify and then redistribute Linux with your modifications, you are required by the license to submit your amendments for possible future versions.

This is how they continually improve and grow without charging our users money. Many Linux users are corporations that use the operating system to run their businesses. Many of these provide fixes and new features for Linux.

Linux is not created and supported by one company, unlike another operating system. It is supported by SUSE, Texas Instruments, Google, Intel, Red Hat, Linaro, Samsung, IBM, AMD, and Microsoft Canonical, and Oracle. Four thousand developers have contributed to Linux over the last 15 years.

UBUNTU MATE WELCOME

It is a utility unique to Ubuntu MATE that helps to guide users with their new operating system. It guides gh post-install configuration, such as installing drivers and adding language support. The welcome guide provides a one-click installation from a highly curated list of best-in-class software to "get stuff done."

- The highlight key features of Ubuntu MATE and GNU/Linux.

- It provides quick guidelines on getting started.

- It provides quick installation guidance.

- It informs users of their system's specifications.

- It links to community forums and social networks.

- It informs of Ubuntu MATE branded products for sale.

- It provides details on donating to the project.

- Software

- You can pick Ubuntu MATE's recommended software tested for the distribution.

- It is simple to manage packages on the system.

- It installs a package manager, such as Ubuntu Software Center.

Plasma 5 provides improved support for HiDPI and migration to Qt5, which takes intensive graphics rendering to GPU, making the CPU faster. Apart from this, Plasma 5 includes a new default theme called Breeze.
Components that make up KDE Plasma 5 include:

1. **Kwin:** Default window manager

2. **Dolphin:** Default file manager

3. **Kwrite/KATE:** Default text editor

4. **Greenview:** Default image viewer

5. **Dragon Player:** Default video player

POWERFUL APPLICATIONS

While MATE Desktop provides the virtual user interfaces to control and use a computer, MATE adds a collection of additional applications to turn your computer into a truly powerful workstation. Naturally, you'll also find a firewall, backup application, document/photo scanner, and printer management, which are all included in Ubuntu MATE.

Ubuntu MATE Welcome

It is a utility unique to Ubuntu MATE that helps to guide users with their new operating system. It guides users through post-install configuration such as installing drivers and adding language support.

Productivity

- MATE uses Firefox to deliver safe and easy web browsing.
- Thunderbird is a featured email client with integrated spam filtering.
- LibreOffice suit is a full-featured office productivity suite compatible with Microsoft(R) Office.

Document Management

- Printing is simple and easy on Ubuntu MATE. In some cases, you can connect your printer via USB cable, and it immediately configures it for use. Printing to a network printer is also easy.
- The Simple Scan application in the Graphics menu provides a simple and easy way to scan documents. The configuration is usually automatic once your scanner is connected via USB or over the network. Load your content, press Scan, then save the image.
- PDF creation on Ubuntu MATE is built-in, whether you are scanning a page, writing a book, or saving a web page. Some applications allow the saving or export of a document as a PDF from the application menus. If any application you use does not offer that directly, you can always print the document as a PDF file.

Entertainment

- **Rhythmbox:** It is a piece of very easy-to-use music playing and organizer.
- **Shotwell:** It is a digital photo organizer.
- **VLC:** By using this you can play, capture, broadcast your multimedia streams.

Games

Ubuntu MATE is compatible with Steam for Linux. Much high-quality and enjoyable open-source game titles are available for Ubuntu MATE via the Ubuntu Software Center.

Security

The MATE is designed with security. It continuously receives updates, ensuring that you have the latest protection for all of your computer's software as soon as it's available.

Accessibility

Making an available operating system was a key priority when the Ubuntu MATE founders set out the project's goals.

Software Centers

There is plenty of additional software available for Ubuntu MATE. Ubuntu MATE's Software Boutique has been created as a carefully curated selection of the best-in-class applications chosen because they integrate well, complement Ubuntu MATE, and enable your computing experience to self-style.

"MATE" came into the picture to differentiate from GNOME 3, yet another desktop environment. It consists of GNOME-originated applications that were earlier part of GNOME 2 and other applications developed from scratch.

Components that make up the MATE Desktop Environment are:

1. **Caja**: default file manager

2. **Pluma**: default text editor

3. **Marco**: window manager

4. **April**: document viewer

5. **Eye of MATE**: image viewer

PRODUCTIVITY APPLICATIONS

Firefox delivers safe, easy web browsing. A familiar user interface enhances security features, including protection from online identity theft, and integrated search lets you get them out of the web.

Thunderbird is a fully featured email, RSS, and newsgroup client that makes emailing safer, faster, and more accessible than ever before. It supports different mail accounts (POP, IMAP, and Gmail). It has a simple mail account setup wizard, one-click address book, tabbed interface, an integrated learning spam filter, advanced search, indexing capabilities, easy organization of mails with tagging and virtual folders, and many more features. It also features unrivaled extensibility.

LibreOffice is a full-featured productivity office suite that replaces Microsoft(R) Office. The clean interface and powerful tools let you unleash your creativity and grow your productivity. LibreOffice embeds some applications that make it the most powerful free and open-source office suite on the market.

- About LibreOffice
  - (Writer), the word processor
  - (Calc), the spreadsheet application
  - (Impress) the presentation engine
  - (Draw) the drawing and flowcharting application
  - (Base), the database and database frontend
  - (Math), for editing mathematics

Currently, MATE has essential mobile device support. You can plug in a phone, media player, or digital camera. The device is automatically detected and mounted and can access the files on it or sync content.

Document Management

MATE makes printing, scanning, and saving documents easier than creating them. All the software is preinstalled for the most popular printers and scanners, so setting up your hardware is easy, too.

Printing

Printing on Ubuntu MATE is simple and easy. Ubuntu MATE Linux kernel already provides the most popular printer drivers. In some cases, you can connect your printer via USB cable, and Ubuntu MATE immediately configures it for use. Printing to a network printer is almost as easy.

You can install the HP Linux Imaging and Printing utility from the Ubuntu MATE Welcome application or the Software Boutique for added control.

ENTERTAINMENT APPLICATIONS

Ubuntu MATE comes with pre-installed three significant applications for managing entertainment and media files and subscriptions. If you need more, the Software Centers offer many more to choose from.

Rhythmbox is a very easy-to-use music playing and management program which supports a wide range of audio formats (including mp3 and Ogg). Initially inspired by Apple's iTunes, the current version also supports

Internet Radio, iPod integration, portable audio player support, audio CD burning and CD playback, music sharing, and podcasts.

Shotwell is a digital photo organizer. It allows importing photos from disk or camera, organizing in various ways, viewing in full-window or full-screen mode, and exporting them to share with others. It can manage a lot of different image formats, including raw CR2 files. For help topics on this application, see the Shotwell manual.

Built-In Security

Another powerful security feature of Ubuntu MATE is that its users are not administrators by default. Administrators on any system have permission to do anything, including the ability to damage the system.

For example, other systems look at the name of a file to determine which program should open it, then immediately open it. This design makes it easy to attack a system. MATE opens a file based on what the file is, not on its name.

The system provides a warning that the file is not a text file but a program that will be run if you permit it to continue. To add extra security, MATE requires you to provide your administrator password before that permission is granted.

Other Various Applications

MATE is composed of several applications. The changes in the name are necessary to avoid conflicts with other GNOME components.

Caja

It is the official file manager for the MATE Desktop. It allows for browsing directories and previewing files, launching applications associated with them, and is also responsible for managing the icons on the MATE Desktop. It works on local and remote file systems. It is a fork of Nautilus.

Pluma

It is a text editor which supports most basic editor features. It also extends the basic functionality with other features not usually found in simple text editors. It is a graphical application that supports editing multiple text files in one window. It fully supports international text by using the Unicode UTF-8 encoding in edited files. Its core feature set includes syntax highlighting source code, auto-indentation, and printing support. It is a fork of Gedit.

April

It is a simple multi-page document viewer. It can display PostScript, Encapsulated PostScript, DJVU, DVI, XPS, and PDF (Portable Document Format) files. The document also allows searching for text, copying text to the clipboard, hypertext navigation, and table-of-contents bookmarks when supported by the document. April is a fork of Evince.

Why Ubuntu MATE?

Ubuntu MATE is a desktop distribution of GNU/Linux and is a dependable, secure, capable computer system that rivals others in popularity and usage.

MATE Terminal

It is a terminal application that can access a UNIX shell in the MATE environment. It can run any application designed to run on VT102, VT220, and xterm terminals. MATE Terminal can also use multiple terminals in a single window (tabs) and support different configurations (profiles) management. MATE Terminal is a fork of GNOME Terminal.

Unlike other operating systems, Linux is used:

- It is the fastest and most powerful supercomputers

- The computers that make up the backbone of the internet

- It servers that require stability and reliability

The Ubuntu MATE is more secure and better supported than the operating system preinstalled on most home computers today.

Using MATE provides for a complete, full-featured operating system, pre-configured with most of the applications you will need for your daily purposes.

Xubuntu
What Is Xubuntu?

It is an Ubuntu-based Linux operating system. It is an easy-to-use operating system and elegant and comes with Xfce, a stable, light, and configurable desktop environment.

It is perfect who want to make the most use of their desktops, laptops, and netbooks, also featuring a modern look and enough features for efficient, daily usage and working well on older hardware.

The "X" stands for Xfce, the desktop environment in Xubuntu, and the word "Ubuntu" denotes the dependency on usage of the Ubuntu core, which also represents the core of the operating system.

Learning more about Xubuntu

Free Software   The Xubuntu project is committed to the principles of free software development people are encouraged to use free software, improve, and pass it on.

Linux   The kernel is the heart of the Xubuntu system. It is an essential part of any operating system, providing the communication bridge between hardware and software.

Xfce   It is the lightweight desktop environment used in Xubuntu and aims to be fast and low on system resources while still visually appealing and user-friendly. It embodies the traditional UNIX philosophy of modularity and reusability.

Getting to Know Your Desktop Environment   After entering your login data, your system booting up will arrive at the Xubuntu desktop. It comes with features designed to make one's life easy, and it is well worth taking the time to get to know it.

Desktop   The Xubuntu desktop has a panel located at the top of the screen.

The Panel   It is used for switching applications, receiving information about the system. On the left side, you will see the Xubuntu logo. Clicking on the icon will open the menu, where you have many choices of applications. Along the bottom of the menu are icons for Settings, Lock Screen, and Log Out.

The middle section is represented as window buttons for open applications. On the right is the clock, displaying the date-time. To the left is the Notification Area. Here you will see indicators that give you information on your system, including network connectivity, sound volume level, battery status, and instant messages. Some notification icons only appear when required, for example, when software updates are available. The panel's position, the items it contains, and the menu are all customizable.

The Desktop   The default desktop has just three icons: Home, File System, and Trash. You can customize your desktop by right-clicking in a blank area and choosing Desktop Settings. Here, you can modify the wallpaper, the menu, and icon behavior.

Files and Directories   Xubuntu comes with Xfce's file manager, Thunar. Load it from > Accessories > File Manager by double-clicking the Home or on File System icon on your desktop.

Navigation   The Manager view consists of a shortcut pane on the left side, the central area on the right, and a path bar. The pane provides shortcuts to other folders on your system.

Removable Devices   When you insert CDs, USB sticks, or other removable media into the system or removable devices like a music player, MATE can automatically detect the new device. For example, after inserting an empty CD into your drive, you will see a shortcut in the left of the File Manager representing the CD.

Features   When we compare Ubuntu MATE to Ubuntu, it is straightforward to decide which is better as long as you understand what is important to you when choosing a desktop environment. In my opinion, there are two relevant, main criteria for determining what desktop environment is better: system resource usage, yielding to traditional metaphors, or tracking innovations.

If you are interested in the lower end of system resource usage, then Ubuntu MATE is more suitable; similarly, if you are primarily interested in a desktop environment that uses traditional metaphors, then Ubuntu MATE is more appropriate.

UNITY

Unity is Ubuntu's default desktop environment. If you have installed Ubuntu using the installer, use the Unity desktop right now.

Unity is Ubuntu's vision of what a Linux desktop should be. In fact, for most users, Unity is probably synonymous with Ubuntu. From its searchable Dash to its application that functions similar to Windows 7 taskbar, Unity has its own identity as a desktop. However, it also includes a variety of programs from the GNOME Desktop. Before Unity, Ubuntu used many GNOME programs, like the Nautilus file manager, which are still used on Unity today.

If you are not using Ubuntu locally, you can play with Unity in the browser using the Ubuntu online website. Its guide is targeted at new Unity users but experienced Ubuntu users might discover a few new tricks.

Features

- **The Unity launcher:** The Unity desktop is the left-aligned launcher. A point in the Unity experience, it allows you to launch, manage, and interact with applications whether they're running or not.

- **The Vertical Launcher:** was designed to effectively use screen space, which was often limited in terms of height than width. Despite repeated user requests, the Unity launcher could not be moved for a long time. Ubuntu LTS made it possible to move the Unity launcher to the bottom of the screen. This one request has been acceded to a bit sooner.

- **The HUD:** The Unity HUD, which stands for Heads-up Display, is as innovative today as when it debuted in Ubuntu 12.04 LTS. The HUD makes finding hidden menu entries deliciously quick. Tap the Alt key and enter a keyword or two, select the right result from the list and hit enter or return to action it.

- **The Dash:** The Unity Dash is a partial application launcher, part file search and part search engine. It lets you find and open locally installed applications, search through your files and folders from one unified window via the Home scope.

It is interesting how the Dash grew over the years, debuting with the version you were most familiar with back in 2012.

The original Unity Dash has a "start page" consisting of four "Places" shortcuts and four links to default apps. The Dash page later integrated app and file history to provide a more useful starting point.

- **Launching a program on the launcher with the Super key**

  - ubuntu-unity-Hotbar: Saving a program on the Unity launcher allows a user to launch it instantly. However, most might not know that each program on the Unity dock is numbered, one through nine precisely. Pressing the Super key (Windows key) + 1 through 9 will instantly launch one of the programs in the Unity launcher.

It means if you want to open the file manager, it is possible to do it instantly by pressing "Super + 1" and so on.

- **Using the Super key (launch specific lenses)**

  - ubuntu-unity-files-lense: Unity has a feature called "lenses," and this feature allows Unity Dash to filter out certain things and search for them. The Music lens searches for music, the Pictures lens searches for photos, and so on. It turns out it possible to have the Unity Dash open directly to any of the pre-installed lenses on Ubuntu.

    1. Super + A: Apps lens

    2. Super + F: Files lens

    3. Super + M: Music lens

    4. Super + C: Photo lens

    5. Super + V: Videos lens

- **Using the Super key (open the trash)**

  - ubuntu-unity-trash: Much like how the Super key can be used to launch specific apps in the launcher, it can open the Trash folder too. By pressing the "Super + T" key launches the Trash folder with Unity. It is handy because it saves time. There's no need to click the Trash icon – just "Super + T" to get to the Trash!

- **Progress bars and badges**

  - **Ubuntu Unity launcher badges and progress bar**: For supported apps, the Unity launcher can display a badge count on launcher items to relay information, like the number of unread emails, new tweets, or concurrent downloads.

  Progress bars are also placed over the launcher item to show the progress of downloads, exports, and renders.

  I hope this feature is added to GNOME Shell or integrated into extensions like Dash to Dock.

- **Global menu:** The global app menu in Unity has signature features in the Ubuntu Netbook edition and has migrated to the desktop with the rest of the Unity Shell in Ubuntu 11.04.

- **Shortcut overlay:** Many of you may not know that the Unity desktop contains an informative list of keyboard shortcuts. This cheat sheet for keyboard enthusiasts lists Unity keyboard shortcuts so that you can learn or recap how to interact with parts of the Unity desktop without needing to take your hands off of the keyboard. To reveal the shortcut overlay, just long-press the Super key.

- **Unity Lenses:** Lenses were dedicated content-specific panels that can add to extend the functionality of the Dash.

  Lenses serve up results from online services and surface local results. Right-clicking on a result in the Dash opens a preview pane with some extra information, content, snippets, music files, or even in-Dash player controls.

  Ubuntu has various Lenses by default over the years, with the current line-up comprising: Apps, Home, Documents, Music, Photos, and Videos. Developers created additional lenses, including ones for YouTube, Tomboy notes, and contacts.

- **Unity 2D:** Unity 2D is the oft-forgotten version of Unity aimed at lower-end devices and virtual machines but adored by desktop users anyway!

- **Smart Scopes:** The Smart Scopes are context-aware searches for the Unity Dash. They allow you to search for "Doctor Who" in the Home Scope and, via the power of a "smart server" backend, see relevant results from popular websites, web services, and locally installed applications. On paper, Unity Smart Scopes should have a game-changer.

- **Chameleonic tendencies:** A Unity feature that some never notice is its chameleonic tendencies. The color of the Unity launcher, the Dash, and notification bubbles change hue based on the dominant color in the background wallpaper.

  There is probably a very complex algorithm at play here, deciding which color in the background is dominant and extracting a suitable hue based on it.

- **Workspaces:** Ubuntu includes multiple workspaces. Each workspace is its desktop, allowing you to group application windows. To view workspaces, click the Workspace Switcher icon on the launcher.

  You can see a review of your workspaces and the windows open on each one. You can switch between workspaces from anywhere.

  You can drag and drop windows on the Workspace Switcher to rearrange your workspaces.

  You can use the Ctrl-Alt-Arrow Key keyboard shortcuts to switch workspaces and probably the quickest, most efficient way to switch workspaces.

- **Indicator menus:** Many essential functions are located in the indicator menus at the top-right corner of your screen. If you want to switch users, shut down your computer, control the volume level, or change network settings, you will get an option in the indicator menus.

  The main icon represents the messaging indicator, which groups new messages for email, instant messaging, and social networking applications into a single icon. The icon turns blue when you have a new message.

  You can use the Ctrl-Alt-Shift-Arrow Key keyboard shortcuts to move windows between workspaces and the same combination of switches between workspaces brings the currently focused window with you.

- **Switching between applications:** The Alt-Tab shortcut switches between applications in Unity, =. When you use the Alt-Tab, it only switches between windows on your active workspace.

  The Alt-Tab switcher groups the applications with multiple windows into an icon. The three arrows to the left indicate that you have three Firefox windows open.

  If you use Alt-Tab and pause with the Firefox icon selected, you will switch between the open Firefox windows. You can skip the screen with the Alt -` keyboard shortcut.

- **Hidden global menus:** Unity uses global menu application menus that are not located in the application windows. They're located on the top panel and might be confusing because you cannot see the application menu until you mouse over the top panel.

When you maximize the window, each window's title bars merge into the top panel and include the window manager controls. When an application window is minimized, maximized, close, and restore buttons are located at the left side of the top panel, above the Dash icon.

- **Keyboard shortcuts cheat sheet:** Unity has many keyboard shortcuts, but you do not need to remember each of them. Just press and hold the Super (i.e., Windows) key, and you will see the keyboard shortcuts cheat sheet, and you will also see numbers over the application icons on the launcher. Use these numbers combined with the Super key to switch to or launch applications.

KUBUNTU

Kubuntu is an entirely open-source operating system built around the Linux kernel. The Kubuntu community is accomplished around the ideals glorified in the Ubuntu philosophy:

- Software should be available free of charge.
- People should use software tools in their local language despite any disabilities.
- All users should have the freedom to customize and alter their software in whatever way they see fit.

Some essential points about Kubuntu:

- It always is free of charge, and there is no extra fee for its "enterprise edition," we make our work available to everyone on the same terms.
- It includes the very best accessibility and translations infrastructure that the free community offers to other users.
- A new release is made every six months, and you can use the current stable release or explore the recent development release. Every single release is supported for at least 18 months.
- It is entirely committed to open-source software development; we inspire people to use open-source software, improve it, and pass it on.

What Is Ubuntu Cinnamon Remix?

Ubuntu Cinnamon is a community-driven remix of Linux distro Ubuntu, combining Linux Mint's flag-ship Cinnamon Desktop with Ubuntu, packed with everything you need. Keeping stability, speed, and elegance is our top priority.

It takes the more traditional approach of a GNOME 2 and MATE-like desktop. It is similar to Windows 7, easy to transition from your Windows system to Ubuntu Cinnamon Remix. Even if you like to keep Windows on the side, you can always dual-boot Windows and Ubuntu Cinnamon Remix.

Using Ubuntu Cinnamon Remix will get the traditional default Cinnamon desktop and most GNOME Desktop applications. The LibreOffice suite also comes preinstalled.

However, all of these are functionalities, so if you want to install any application that does something for you, such as a firewall, you can uninstall the old firewall.

In other words, Cinnamon gives you the standardized and traditional software that allows the user to remove the application and choose a different application.

Ubuntu Cinnamon Remix.

Install Cinnamon from Ubuntu Repositories

If you want to install Cinnamon on Ubuntu running 20.04 LTS or newer, here's what to do. First, open a terminal window on the Ubuntu desktop. The terminal window will open by pressing Ctrl + Alt + T (or Ctrl + Shift + T) on the keyboard; follow the steps below:

- Cinnamon is available for all Ubuntu users via the software repository. However, not all users have access to "Universe" out of the box, so we will demonstrate how to set it up.

- The Cinnamon environment is separated into several different packages. They are all tied together via the "Cinnamon desktop environment." So, if you want to get the complete Cinnamon experience on Ubuntu, you must install this package.

- Run the given command to install the Cinnamon desktop:

  - $ sudo apt install cinnamon-desktop-environment

  - Allow the Cinnamon to install on your Ubuntu PC. It will take some time. Reboot your PC when the installation process is complete.

  - You will see the login screen when your system turns on. Click "log out" to exit the session.

Features of Cinnamon

- The Desktop effects, animations, transition effects, and transparency using composition

- Panels equipped with a main menu, launchers, a window list, and the system tray can be adjusted on the left, right, the upper or lower edge of the screen

- Various extensions

- Applets appear on the panel

- The Overview with functions similar to the GNOME Shell

- Easy customization of the editor settings

- Customizability of the desktop effects, applets, extensions, the panel, the calendar, themes

- Using the scroll wheel, you can adjust volume and brightness while pointing at the respective taskbar icon

There is no official documentation for Cinnamon, although most documentation for GNOME Shell applies to Cinnamon.

Components that make up this environment are:

1. Muffin is the default window manager.

2. Nemo is the default file manager.

3. gedit is the default text editor.

4. Eye of GNOME is the default image viewer.

5. Totem is the default video player.

Reasons for Using Cinnamon

1. It has a crisp, clean look that uses easy-to-read fonts and color combinations. The desktop is not hampered. You can configure the icons are shown on the desktop using the Settings => Desktop menu. It allows specifying whether the desktop icons are offered only on the primary monitor, secondary monitors, or all.

2. Cinnamon is fast, and programs load and display fast. The desktop loads quickly during login, though this is my subjective experience and is not based on timed testing.

3. The Cinnamon Panel is initially configured very simply, i.e., the toolbar. It contains the menu to launch programs, a system tray, and an application selector. The panel is used efficiently to configure, adding new program launchers to locate the program in the main menu; right-click Select "Add to panel" add the launcher icon to the desktop and the Cinnamon "Favorites" launcher bar. You can enter the Edit mode and rearrange the icons.

4. Like other desktop environments, it offers multiple desktops, and Cinnamon calls these "workspaces." The workspace selector is located on the panel and shows the outlines of the windows located

on each workspace. Windows can be moved between workspaces or assigned to all, but some found that the workspace selector is sometimes slow.

5. Most desktops use their preferred default applications for various purposes. We preferred desktop file manager is Krusader, but Cinnamon uses Nemo as default. Some users like Nemo. It has an excellent clean interface and is frequently used by users. It is easy to use and flexible enough. Hence, Nemo is a fork of Nautilus. The Nautilus interface seems to be poorly integrated.

6. It can be challenging to locate a minimized or hidden running application. So the most useful favorite feature is to drag the buttons for the running applications and rearrange them.

7. The desktop also has an excellent pop-up menu that you can access with a right click. That menu has selections for some frequently used tasks such as accessing the Desktop Settings and adding Desklets and other desktop-related jobs.

Cinnamon is a fork of GNOME, and it is the default desktop environment on Linux Mint and MATE.

Other minor projects and components integrated into the Cinnamon desktop comprisethe following:

1. **MDM display manager**: It is a program that provides graphical login capabilities Ubuntu distribution. It can control the user sessions and manage user authentication.

2. **Nemo file manager**: Nemo is the default file manager of Mint and is a fork of file manager GNOME. Mint has improvised a number of things in its distribution, with two notable among them being Cinnamon and Nemo.

Xfce Desktop Environment

A DE is a collection of the window manager, icons, panels, etc. It determines the look of GUI you will get on your distro. It includes other software, including file managers and others. We have various choices like KDE, Unity, GNOME, Xfce, etc. Now we will discuss Xfce.

Xfce Desktop Environment

It is a desktop environment for the X window system for UNIX-based systems. It has been about for more than two decades, and it has changed a lot and was rewritten two times. The latest version was released in 2015.

It has various features which we will discuss one by one.

1. **Modular:** It is based on the UNIX of modularity and reusability. It is a modular DE, a collection of various modules rather than a single package. It means that you can also install an individual module of Xfce, such as its file manager, without the complete package.

2. **Lightweight:** Xfce is lxde in terms of minimal resource usage. It performs GNOME and KDE to a large extent. Its aim is to reduce resource usage, which is many distros like Linux lite can use it. It helps to bring back the old system to the new.

3. **Appearance:** Xfce might be old, but it is modern in its look and feel. It is used in many other Linux distributions. It gives customization to make it look like a different DE.

4. **Stability:** Xfce can be called the most stable DE. But now there is also a problem with that. Its updates are available once a year or more and do not change much. It is written with gtk+ based on C. Xfce recently is trying to rewrite its code to gtk3. Some components are available in gtk3, while others are still in the developmental stages. Gtk is open-source, and GNOME uses the same.

5. **User-friendly:** It has a valuable panel for Windows users and has a dock for Mac users. Mint has Cinnamon as the main advantage over Ubuntu in getting windows users. The Cinnamon has bugs and is developed keeping mint in mind, whereas Xfce is for all distros. Freedesktop.org publishes the desktop standards. It tries to follow the paths laid down by those standards. These standards are one of the main priorities of Xfce development.

INSTALL XFCE DESKTOP ON UBUNTU

Linux distributions like Xubuntu, Manjaro, OpenSUSE, Zenwalk, and others provide their Xfce desktop packages.

Hence, you can install the latest version with the following commands:

$ sudo apt update

$ sudo apt install xfce4

Wait for the installation to complete, then log out of your current session, or you can restart your system. At the login, choose Xfce desktop and log in.

Removing Xfce Desktop in Ubuntu and Fedora

If you do not want Xfce desktop on your system, use the commands below to uninstall it:

$ sudo apt purge Xubuntu-icon-theme xfce4-*

$ sudo apt autoremove

CORE COMPONENTS OF XFCE DE

Modern DEs are not simple window managers and icon collections anymore. They grew to accommodate many other components that provide a complete desktop experience.

The following components belong to Xfce DE:

1. **File manager**: It is handled by Thunar. It is, just like all the components of the Xfce, developed from scratch by the Xfce team. The interface is minimal and can still be customized to a great extent. It does not provide many options, but we will not use them. It is simple and easy.

2. **Window manager**: It is an app that manages all the windows. xfwm is the default and can be replaced by others like Fluxbox. It has a terminal, libraries, CD burner, and other projects that are designed to be light on system resources and flexible on the configuration part. The critical task is the Xfce settings manager. It provides a configuration that new users sometimes feel confused about. But it is helpful for experienced users.

3. **Xfwm**: It is a compositing window manager.

4. **Thunar**: The file manager, which resembles Nautilus but is more efficient and fast.

5. **Orage**: It is the default calendar application for Xfce.

6. **Mousepad**: It is a file editor that initially forked from Leafpad but is now being actively developed and maintained from scratch.

7. **Parole**: It is a media player based on the Gstreamer framework made for Xfce.

8. **Xfburn**: It is the CD/DVD burner for Xfce.

Features

It offers a beautiful user interface combined with the following components and features:

- It has Xfwm windows manager.

- It has Thunar file manager and application manager.

- The user session manager to deal with logins, power management, and more.

- The desktop manager for setting a background image, desktop icons, and many more.

- It is highly pluggable as well, plus several other features.

CHAPTER SUMMARY

In this chapter, we talked about the various desktop environments of the Ubuntu system along with their features, why we use these environments, and also talked about the various components of each desktop environment.

CHAPTER 4

Ubuntu Linux Apps

IN THIS CHAPTER

➤ Introduction

➤ Various Ubuntu applications

In the previous chapter, we discussed the various desktop environments with their features and the various components of each desktop environment.

Now we will look at the best applications for Ubuntu, which you will find very useful.

INTRODUCTION

Software like Firefox, LibreOffice, and Thunderbird is not featured if you already have them installed. Many users who have switched to Ubuntu from Microsoft Windows or other operating system face the dilemma of finding the best alternative to application software they have been using for years on their previous OS. Ubuntu has thousands of free-to-use and open-source application software that performs way better than many paid software's on Windows and other OS.

The following list features much application software in various categories to find the best application that best matches your requirements.

DOI: 10.1201/9781003311997-4

GEARY EMAIL CLIENT APPLICATION

The above picture makes a clear pitch of Geary email client.

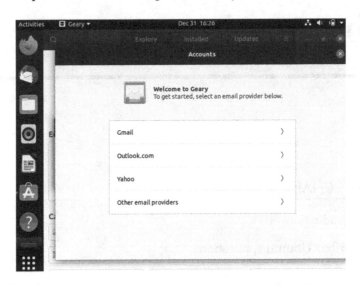

Geary email client application.

As a Gmail user, you can tend to read, write, and send email in a browser tab because it's simple, fast, and works the same across most systems. But the Geary email client above makes a persuasive pitch for using a dedicated desktop email app.

Geary is a fully-featured IMAP email client that gets you set up to send and receive mail from famous webmail providers, including Gmail, Outlook, etc. It does things quickly. It can integrate with GNOME Online Accounts, which you can access from the Settings > Online Accounts panel. Once you're set up and synced with your email provider, you'll find that Geary offers a clean, modern look for your mail and offers good integration with the GNOME Shell desktop.

Powerful mail search features an email composer and many other features like its "conversation" based email threading. You can install Geary on Ubuntu easily by using a dedicated desktop email app from Ubuntu Software.

If you want to use the most up-to-date version of Gear, you will need to install the app from Flathub.

GOOGLE CHROME BROWSER APPLICATION

Almost every Linux distribution features Mozilla browser by default, and it is a tough competitor to Chrome. But Chrome has more advantages over Firefox. It gives direct access to your Google account from where you can sync bookmarks, browser history, extensions, etc., using Chrome browser on other operating systems and mobile phones.

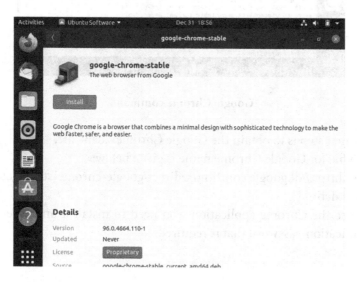

Google Chrome.

Google Chrome has features to update Flash player for Linux, which is not with other web browsers on Linux, including Firefox and Opera browser. If you continually use Chrome on Windows, it is best to use it on Linux.

Installing Google Chrome Using the Command Line

From the command line take a couple of commands to install Google Chrome. We will use the wget command to download the ".deb" file. The Ubuntu package manager uses installation packages called ".deb" files.

Google Chrome command.

The first step is to obtain the Google Chrome ".deb" file.

.deb file for Google Chrome name is given below:

wget https://dl.google.com/linux/direct/google-chrome-stable_current _amd64.deb

To use the Chrome application, you need to install it and enter your authentication password that is required.

Authentication required for installation.

Updating Google Chrome

Google Chrome adds a repository that the apt command checks when looking for installation files. So, Ubuntu doesn't have Google Chrome in any standard repositories, and you can still use apt to upgrade Chrome.

The command to use is:

```
$ sudo apt install google-chrome-stable
```

It will install Google Chrome. The apt command realizes that Chrome is already installed. It will check the available version in the repository and the version installed on your computer. If the performance in the repository is newer than the version on your computer, the more recent version will install for you.

If you run this command after you have installed Google Chrome, the version in the repository and the version on your computer will be updated if needed so that nothing will happen.

STEAM APPLICATION

Game playing on Linux is real now. Users earlier were confused about switching to Linux from Windows because they would not be able to play their favorite games on the Ubuntu system, but now that is not the case.

Some users might face difficulty installing Steam on Linux, but it is worth all efforts as thousands of Steam games are available on Linux. Some popular games like Global Offensive, Hitman, and Dota 2 are also available for Linux, and you need to make sure that you have the minimum hardware requirement to play these games.

Install Steam Package

Here is the command to install Steam from the Ubuntu 20.04 base repository:

```
$ sudo apt install steam
```

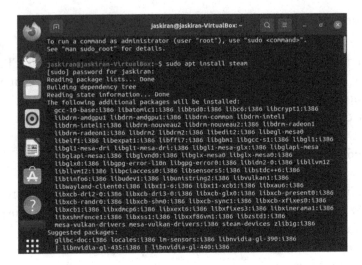

Steam installer.

Once the updates have been downloaded, the following screen will appear.

Steam window.

If you do not have a Steam account to log in, select the "Create New Account" option and enter the correct information in the fields.

If you have an account, click the "Login to An Existing Account" option and enter the username and password in the fields. Steam will send a code to your email address for accessing the account from any unknown device and then enter the security code in the box, and you will be ready to use Steam.

Now, search for your favorite games and enjoy them on Steam.

Enable Multiverse Repository

Ensure that the multiverse repository is enabled before installing Steam from the Ubuntu 20.04 base repository. Run the following command to do so:

```
$ sudo add-apt-repository multiverse
```

Update and Upgrade System

Here is the command to update and upgrade your Ubuntu 20.04 system:

```
$ sudo apt update
```

Launch Steam Application

After installing the Steam application, run the application either from the terminal or the menu. To launch the application from the terminal, run the following command:

```
$ steam
```

Download Steam Debian Package

The official Steam package can be downloaded using the following command:

```
$ wget -O ~/steam.deb http://media.steampowered.com/client/installer/steam.deb
```

Install Steam Using Debian Package

Next, install Steam using the following command:

$ sudo dpkg --install steam.deb

WORDPRESS DESKTOP CLIENT APPLICATION

WordPress has its desktop client for Ubuntu, where you can manage your WordPress sites and can also write and design separately on the desktop client without switching browser tabs.

WordPress backs your websites, and this desktop client is the application for you as you can also keep track of all the WordPress notifications in a single window and check stats for the performance of posts on the website. The desktop client is available in Ubuntu Software Center, from where you can download and install it.

Install WordPress.com Desktop App on Linux

Go and download the client from the site https://apps.wordpress.com/desktop/. For Debian-based distros, there is a deb package and for other Linux distros, download the tar.gz file.

Once you download cd into the download directory, run the following command to install it onto your Linux OS.

For Debian/Ubuntu-Based Distros

The command is given below:

sudo gdebi wordpress*.deb

The file is located at /usr/share/wpcom/wpcom, and to list all files installed by the WordPress.com desktop app, issue this command:

dpkg-query -L wordpress.com

For all others, i.e., Fedora, Arch Linux, OpenSUSE, etc., first extract the tarball.

tar xvf WordPress-com-Linux-x64-1-3-1.tar.gz

A new directory is created under the current directory, .cd under it.

cd WordPress.com-Linux-x64/

You may find an executable called WordPress.com in the same directory. Now you can launch the WordPress app in this way.

./WordPress.com

Another Way to Install WordPress
The following are the steps to install WordPress:

1. Open your Ubuntu software.

2. Search for WordPress and install it in your system.

3. Once the installation is complete, double-click the icon of the WordPress.

4. WordPress window will be once.

VLC MEDIA PLAYER APPLICATION

VLC is a top-rated cross-platform and open-source media player available for Ubuntu. It makes VLC the best media player because it can play videos in audio and video formats.

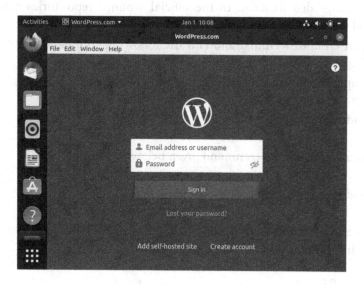

Wordpress VLC media player.

VLC has a user interface that is very easy to use. Apart from that, it offers many features such as online video streaming, audio, video customization, etc.

Install VLC Player as a Snap Package

Snap Package are self-contained packages that include all dependencies needed to run the application. Unlike the standard deb packages, it has a larger disk footprint and longer application startup time. The snap packages are regularly updated with the latest security and bug fixes.

These packages can be installed from the command line or via the Ubuntu Software application.

To install VLC Media Player, open your terminal (Ctrl + Alt + T) and run the following command:

```
$ sudo snap install vlc
```

The VLC snap package will automatically update in the background whenever a new version is released. If you do not want to use the command prompt, open Ubuntu Software, search for "VLC", and install the application.

Installing VLC with apt

The package deb included in the official Ubuntu repositories may lag behind the latest version of VLC.

Open Ubuntu terminal and run the following commands with sudo privileges:

To update your VLC, use the command given below:

```
$ sudo apt update
```

To install VLC use the command given below:

```
$ sudo apt install vlc
```

When a new version is released, you can update VLC through the command line or your desktop Software Update tool.

Starting VLC

In the search bar, type "VLC" and click on the icon of the VLC application.

When you start the player for the first time, a window like the one shown in Figure will appear.

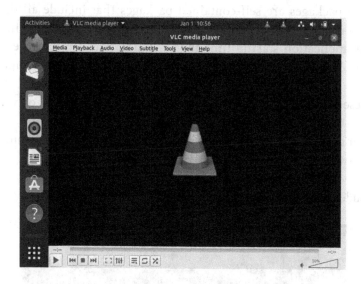

VLC media player.

Set VLC as the Default Media Player

If you want to set it as the default media player, open the Activities screen, search for "Default Applications", and click on it.

When the "Default Applications" window opens, in the Music and Videos dropdowns, select "VLC Media Player".

ATOM TEXT EDITOR APPLICATION

Atom is a free and open-source editor which can be used as Integrated Development Environment (IDE) for coding and editing in primary programming languages.

Atom Text is one of the best user interfaces. It is a feature-rich text editor with offerings like auto-completion, syntax highlighting, and support of extensions and plug-ins.

It shows two ways of installing Atom on Ubuntu 20.04. Atom can be installed as a snap package via the Snapcraft store or as a deb package from the Atom repositories.

Choose the installation that is most suitable for your environment. The exact instructions apply for any Ubuntu-based distribution, including Kubuntu, Linux Mint, and Elementary OS.

Installing Atom as a Snap Package

Github maintains the Atom snap package.

Snap packages are self-contained packages that include all dependencies needed to run the application. It has a larger disk footprint and longer application startup time than the standard deb packages. The snap packages are regularly updated with the latest security and bug fixes.

These packages can be installed from the command line or via the Ubuntu Software application.

To install the Atom snap, open your terminal (Ctrl + Alt + T) and run the following command:

$ sudo snap install atom –classic

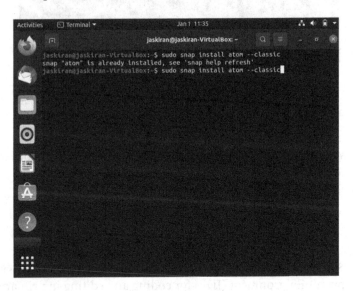

Atom editor installation using command.

Installing Atom with apt

It is available from the APT repositories. To install it, follow the steps below:

You can update the packages list and install the dependencies:

$ sudo apt update

Starting Atom

Type "Atom" in the Activities search bar, type "Atom", and click on the icon to launch the application.

When you start the Atom editor for the first time, a window like the following should appear.

Atom editor window.

You can start installing themes, adding extensions, configuring the editor according to your preferences.

GIMP PHOTO EDITOR APPLICATION

GIMP (GNU Image Manipulation Program) is a free, open-source photo editor for Ubuntu. It is the best alternative to Adobe Photoshop on Windows. If you continuously use Adobe Photoshop and find it difficult to get used to GIMP, you can customize GIMP to look similar to Photoshop.

It is a feature-rich editor, and you can always use additional features by installing extensions and plug-ins anytime.

GIMP released its GIMP 2.10, six years after the last major release of version 2.8. The next major release is GIMP 3.0 but is still under development. Here is the first window of GIMP when you installed it.

GIMP window.

Install GIMP in Ubuntu and Other Linux Distributions

GIMP 2.10 should now be available for most Linux distributions. In Ubuntu, you can find the snap of GIMP in the Software Center and install it from there.

Installing GIMP via Snap Packages

You can use the Snap package for installing GIMP. If you are using Ubuntu, ensure that you have Snap support enabled for other Linux distributions.

Use the following Snap command to install the GIMP in your Ubuntu system:

$ sudo snap install gimp.

Use the Snap command to update the GIMP in your Ubuntu system:

$ sudo apt update

Use the Snap apt command to install the GIMP in your Ubuntu system:

$ sudo apt install gimp

Get GIMP Source Code

Alternatively, you can always install GIMP from the source code. You should download the source code from the link below:

https://download.gimp.org/mirror/pub/gimp/v2.10/

GIMP Source Code

GIMP is an essential tool for graphic designers using Linux. It is capable of doing everything from a professional photo editor. It requires learning, of course.

GOOGLE PLAY MUSIC DESKTOP PLAYER APPLICATION

Google Play Music Player is an open-source music player that is a replica of Google Play Music.

You need to sign in into Google account, and then it will import all your music and favorites into this desktop client. You can download installation files from its official website and install them using Software Center.

It is now officially known as GPMDP (GPMDP). If you would like to use Google Play Music on Ubuntu, you will learn about the multiple ways to install the latest Google Play Music Manager.

Some features of Google Play Music Manager (GPMM):

- It offers an in-built audio equalizer option and mini player.

- It supports playing.

- It has FM scrobbling.

- It supports various media keys like Play, Stop, Pause, etc.

- You can play music in the background.

Install GPMDP Using Flatpak

We can also use Flatpak to install Google Play Music Manager. Ubuntu versions come with Flatpak but if your system doesn't have it, then use the following command in the terminal:

$ sudo apt install flatpak

While installation, it will require permission to continue to install Flatpak, so press Y to continue. Now, execute the command to download all the needed packages for Flatpak. Here is the first window of the Google Play Music.

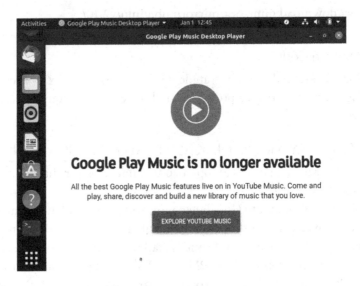

Google Play Music.

Google Play Music is now no longer available; you can check YouTube music just by clicking the button.

Install GPMDP Using Snap Packages

In case you do not have snap, then use the below command to install it easily:

$ sudo apt install snap

and to update apt then you can run the following command:

$ sudo apt update

FRANZ APPLICATION

An instant messaging client combines chat and messaging services into a single application. It is the modern instant messaging platform, and it supports WhatsApp, Facebook Messenger, Skype, Telegram, WeChat, and Google Hangouts under one single application.

It is a messaging platform that you can use for businesses to manage mass customer service.

To install Franz messaging application, you need to download the installation package from the official website and open it using Software Center.

It is a cross-platform app available for Windows, Linux, and macOS. As for the Linux platform, Franz is officially known as a DEB and an AppImage. Linux Mint, based on Ubuntu, can handle the DEB package. Moreover, it's available as a Flatpak. There are multiple methods of getting Franz. Now, Franz isn't free of charge.

Install Franz using DEB package

First, we need to go to the official DEB site, go to the Franz download section and download the package from this link: https://meetfranz.com/ #download

Click the "Ubuntu" button. It'll directly start downloading the Franz DEB package.

We are now installing it using APT. Launch the terminal and get started with the installation. First, update your apt-cache.

$ sudo apt update

Now, install the DEB package.

$ sudo apt install ./franz_5.4.0_amd64.deb (version name can be vary)

Install Franz using Flatpak

Flatpak is a Linux package, and it will run on any Linux distro given the support for the Flatpak package manager. Check the Flatpak official website.

In the case of Linux Mint, it is supported by default. We can perform Franz's installation.

To install Franz in your Ubuntu system, run the below command in the terminal:

$ sudo apt update && sudo apt install Flatpak

SYNAPTIC PACKAGE MANAGER APPLICATION

Synaptic is a lightweight front-end GUI apt package management system used in Ubuntu, Linux Mint, and many other Debian or Ubuntu-based distributions.

It is one of the Ubuntu tools because it works for graphical interfaces for a command like "apt-get", which we use to install Ubuntu apps using terminal. It gives really tough competition to default app stores various Linux distros.

Synaptic Package Manager Features

Here is full list of what you can do with Synaptic:

- It updates the package cache.

- It upgrades the entire system.

- It manages package repositories.

- It can search for packages by name, description, maintainer, version, dependencies, etc.

- It lists packages by section, status (installed), origin, or more.

- It sorts packages by name, status, size, or version.

- It gets information related to a package.

- It can lock package version.

- It can install a specific version of a package.

The Synaptic package is available in the repository in Ubuntu. If it is enabled, you may find it in the Software Center.

Installing Synaptic Package Manager

To install Synaptic package manager, open the terminal on your system and enter the command:

$ sudo apt install synaptic

Enter the password, press Y, and then Enter.

Once the installation gets complete, you can open the GUI window by typing

$ sudo synaptic

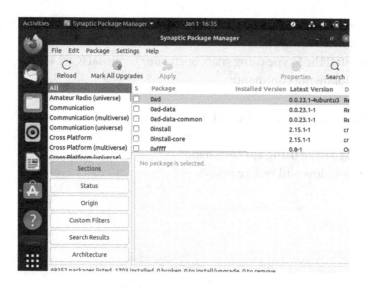

Synaptic package manager.

You can search for the required packages in the search bar placed at the top.

To remove your synaptic package manager you can use the below command:

$ sudo apt remove synaptic

SKYPE APPLICATION

Skype is a cross-platform video calling application that is now also available for Linux as a Snap app. It is an instant messaging application that offers features like voice and video calls, desktop screen sharing, etc.

It has a fantastic interface similar to the desktop client on Windows and is very easy to use. It could be a handy app for many switchers from Windows.

$ sudo snap install skype

Snap packages are self-contained packages that include all dependencies needed to run the application. It has a larger disk footprint and longer application startup time than the standard deb packages. The snap packages are regularly updated with the latest security and bug fixes.

These packages can be installed from the command line or via the Ubuntu Software application.

To install the Skype using snap, open your terminal (Ctrl + Alt + T) and run the following command:

$ sudo snap install skype --classic

Installing Skype using apt command
First window will be like below.

File Edit View Tools Help

Welcome to Skype

Free HD video and voice calls anywhere in the world.

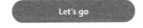

Skype window.

Skype is now available from the official Microsoft APT repositories. To install it, follow the steps given below.

Open your terminal and download the Skype.deb package using the following wget command:

wget https://go.skype.com/skypeforlinux-64.deb

Once the download of the deb file is complete, install Skype by running the following command as a user with sudo privileges:

$ sudo apt install./skypeforlinux-64.deb

Then, enter your authentication system password.

The official Skype will be added to your system during the installation process. When a new version is released, you can update the Skype package using the desktop standard Software Update tool or simply running the following commands in your terminal.

To update your apt use the command given below:

```
$ sudo apt update
```

To upgrade your apt use the command is given below:

```
$ sudo apt upgrade
```

VIRTUALBOX APPLICATION

It is a cross-platform virtualization software application developed by Oracle Corporation. You can try Linux, Mac inside Windows System, or Windows and Mac inside Linux.

It creates a virtual drive and installs a guest operating system on it. You can download and install VB directly from Ubuntu Software Center.

Install VirtualBox from Ubuntu Repositories

The one way to install VirtualBox is by using the official Ubuntu repositories.

Open a terminal, and then enter the following to update the repository:

```
$ sudo apt-get update
```

Download and install VirtualBox by running

```
$ sudo apt-get install VirtualBox
```

Next, install the VirtualBox Extension Pack:

```
$ sudo apt-get install VirtualBox—ext–pack
```

Install Latest Version of VirtualBox

Start by updating the package lists:

```
$ sudo apt-get update
```

To Install VirtualBox on Ubuntu, use the command

$ sudo apt-get install VirtualBox

It was designed for 64-bit operating systems. If you are running a 32-bit OS, you can use VirtualBox 5.2 instead.

To install VirtualBox, enter the following

$ sudo apt-get install VirtualBox

Ubuntu VirtualBox windows.

Install VirtualBox Extension Pack
The VirtualBox Extension enhances the functionality of your virtual machines. It adds extra tools like USB 2.0 and 3.0, Remote Desktop, and encryption.
Enter the following:

wget https://download.virtualbox.org/virtualbox/6.1.24/Oracle_VM _VirtualBox_Extension_Pack-6.1.24.vbox-extpack.

Using VirtualBox
Launch the VirtualBox by typing the following in the terminal:

$ Virtualbox

After running the VirtualBox command, a graphic interface loads. Click on the Add or New button to create a new virtual machine, and then a dialog box opens where you can select the operating system and version you would like to create, then click Next.

The dialog box will offer you several options for your virtual machine. It will ask you to allocate memory, hard drive, and others to the virtual machine, or you can also use default options if you are not sure about customizing.

A new machine is available on the left side once you finish. Select the new machine and click the green arrow button. A new window will open and boot up the virtual machine.

UNITY TWEAK TOOL APPLICATION

Unity Tweak Tool, a GNOME Tweak Tool, is a must-have tool for every Linux user because it allows users to customize their desktop according to their needs. You can also try new GTK themes, set up your desktop hot corners, customize icon pack, tweak unity launcher, etc.

INSTALLING GNOME TWEAK TOOL

To install the Tweak tool, type the following command:

$ sudo apt-get install gnome-tweak-tool

After getting it, use the command and install the "GNOME tweak tool". Once the tweak tool is installed, you can found in applications, as shown in the following image.

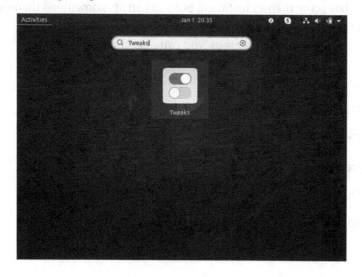

GNOME Tweak icon.

When you hit icon the next window will open given below.

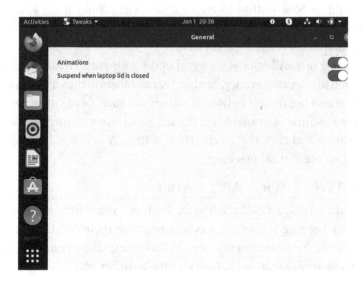

GNOME Tweak window.

Windows usually are animated, whether open or close. You can disable those animations to save battery.

CHANGING THEMES USING THE TWEAK TOOL

Linux allows other various modifications to your desktop appearance. Themes can be changed from the "Appearance" tab. The Tweak tool already has some themes installed, but you can also download themes and install them using this tool.

Apart from changing themes, you can also change the:

1. Background image

2. Lock screen image

3. Cursor

4. Icons

5. Shell

6. Sound

Extensions

The tab is the "Extensions" tab, where you can enable, disable, and add the extensions. Extensions can download easily from the link: https://extensions.gnome.org. It automatically detects the "GNOME tweak tool" and asks for a browser extension to download; download that extension and add. Now download any other extension from the above site, and it will appear in the "Extensions" tab.

Managing Fonts

Fonts can be managed from the "Fonts" tab. Interface, Document, and fonts like Mono-space can also change from here.

Keyboard and Mouse Settings

In the tab "Keyboard & Mouse", you can adjust various settings related to the keyboard, mouse, and trackpad. The thing to be focused on is the touchpad disable option. You can type without any problem with the touchpad when you enable it.

Startup Applications

It would be best to have some applications when you turn on the desktop. You can add applications that immediately start while booting up the operating system from this tab.

Modifying the Top Bar

The further option is modifying the top bar. There are some adjustments that you can make in the top bar, like:

- Enabling the battery percentage

- Modification in clock

- Calendar settings

- Configuring window title bars

Another essential tweaking feature is that it allows you to modify the title bar icons. Apart from that, it permits enabling and disabling the "minimize" and "maximize" buttons on the above title bar.

FLATPAK APPLICATION

It is a utility for software and package management for Linux. It offers a sandbox environment where users can run the application software in separateness from the rest of the system.

It was developed as part of the freedesktop.org project known as X Desktop Group or XDG and was initially called xdg-app.

Features of Flatpak

- It provides a sandboxing environment for running apps.

- It provides support for 24 Linux distros.

- It helps run multiple versions of the same app at the same time.

- There are no dependency incompatibilities.

- The automatic application update in the background.

Enabling Flatpak Support

If you are using Fedora, Endless OS, Linux Mint, CentOS, or Elementary OS, you can skip this step because you do not need to install Flatpak. Most of these Linux distros come with preinstalled and default Flatpak support.

To enable Flatpak on other Linux distributions, we have to run a single command to install Flatpak and autoconfigure with the Linux system.

To install Flatpak on Debian, OS, Ubuntu, and its derivatives, use the following command:

$ sudo apt install flatpak

To install Flatpak on the version of Ubuntu before 18.10, use the following commands:

- sudo apt install flatpak

- sudo apt update

Once you install Flatpak, restart your system, and we are ready to hop on to the next step of Flatpak applications. But before going forward, we will discuss three methods to download and install Flatpak apps from the Flathub repo.

- Installing Flatpak app using command line
- Installing Flatpak apps using GNOME Software Center
- Installing Flatpak apps using.flatpakref file

1. **Installing Flatpak Apps Using GNOME Software Center?**

   - **Install Flatpak Plug-In:** The visual method is the easiest way to install Flaptak apps. To use the Software Center, you must first enable Flatpak support. Hence, if you are using the GNOME desktop environment, install the Flatpak plug-in by running the command:

     $ sudo apt install gnome-software-plugin-flatpak

     For KDE desktop, use this command:

     $ sudo apt install plasma-discover-backend-flatpak

2. **Installing Flatpak Apps Using Flatpak file?**

   Search for App At the Flathub platform and then go to the online Flathub app store and search for your desired app.

   - **Download the .flatpakref Flatpak File:** Click on "Install", and it'll download torrents like flatpak file.flatpakref, which we'll use in the next step to install the app.

   - **Install Flatpak app from .flatpakref File:** Now, execute the app command using the .flatpakref file given below:

     flatpak install --from /path/to/<app-id>.flatpakref

     Once you complete installing the app, you can either search in your system or run the following command to open the app:

     flatpak run <app-id>

3. **How to Install Flatpak Apps Using Command Line?**

   - **Installing the Flathub Repository:** To install a Flatpak app using the terminal, we first need to install the Flathub repository to search for the app and then install it.

So, run the command to add Flathub having the list of applications:

flatpak remote-add --if-not-exists flathub https://flathub.org/ repo/flathub.flatpakrepo

- **Search Flatpak App from Terminal:** We can search any thing using a single command:

$ flatpak search <app-name>

- **Install Flatpak App Using App ID:** Pick the app you want to install, copy its ID, and pass it as input to the following command:

$ flatpak install flathub <app-id>

Now run the application using the command:

flatpak run <app-id>

Flatpak commands

If you want to know more about Flatpak, you can check all its commands by reading the manual page:

$ man flatpak

There are various commands for managing the applications. One is the Flatpak list that displays all installed Flaptak apps on your system.

flatpak list

To update the particular app, you can run:

flatpak update <app-id>

- **Uninstalling Flatpak Apps?:** If you want to remove Flatpak, you can use both graphical and command-line methods.

If using a command line, simply run Flatpak list and grab the app-id. Then, run the following command to uninstall the app:

flatpak uninstall <app-id>

- **Ubuntu Cleaner:** Ubuntu Cleaner is a maintenance tool created to remove packages that are no longer useful, remove unnecessary apps, and clean up browser caches. It has a straightforward user interface that is very easy to use.

How to Install Ubuntu Cleaner in Ubuntu LTS

You can smoothly install Ubuntu Cleaner by adding PPA and installing it.

1. $ sudo apt install software-properties-common

2. $ sudo add-apt-repository PPA:gerardpuig/PPA

3. $ sudo apt update

4. $ sudo apt install ubuntu-cleaner

Run the following command in terminal to remove Ubuntu Cleaner:

$ sudo apt remove ubuntu-cleaner && sudo apt autoremove

COREBIRD APPLICATION

Corebird Twitter client is used as the desktop client. It is the best Twitter client available for Linux that offers features similar to the Twitter app on the mobile phone.

It gives notifications whenever someone likes and retweets your tweets or messages, and you also add multiple Twitter accounts to this client.

How to Install Corebird Twitter Client on Ubuntu

It is a modern, lightweight, and open-source desktop client which can handle accounts and has all the main Twitter features, including Streaming, Favorites, Lists, comprehensive tweet filters, integrated Search, Mentions/ Notifications, timelines, and supports multiple accounts. It shows the installation procedure of the Corebird Twitter client on Ubuntu.

Installation Procedure

Add the dependency package into the repository via PPA to start the installation procedure.

The system has updated the required repositories and executed the following commands to install the Corebird application:

$ apt-get update

$ apt-get install corebird

The Corebird application has been installed successfully in the system. To run the application, type the application name in the Ubuntu dashboard and click on the icon to run the application.

- It automatically opens the browser and asks for the login details of Twitter, fills the required information, and clicks authorize app option.

- The authorization page shows the generated PIN copied and pasted on the Corebird application.

- Paste the copied PIN in the application and click on Confirm option.

- Twitter account is now open and running successfully.

PIXBUF APPLICATION

Pixbuf offers to share, sell, and analyze photos in a better way. It wants to sell itself as a photo manager which can communicate on various social networks.

It is cross-platform with binaries for macOS, Linux, and Windows and also has a mobile application compatible with Android and iOS.

It is a desktop client from the Pixbuf photo community hub that lets you upload, share, and sell your photos and supports photo sharing to social media networks like Instagram, Facebook, Pinterest, Twitter, and photography, including Flickr 500px and Youpic.

It offers analytics features that give you stats about clicks, retweets, repins on your photo, scheduled posts, and a dedicated iOS extension. It has a mobile app so that you can always connect with your Pixbuf account from anywhere. It is also available for download in Ubuntu Software Center as a snap package.

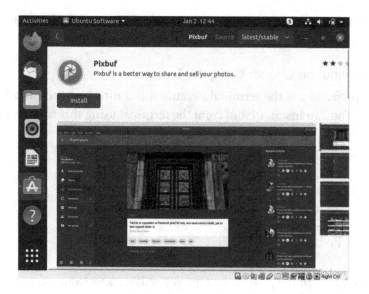

Pixbuf application.

Some features that make Pixbuf are:

- It uploads your photos to several services.

- It resizes your photos and adds metadata.

- It shares your content automatically with your followers

- It supports all major social networks and photography services like Flick, Instagram, Twitter, Pinterest, Facebook.

Install Pixbuf on Ubuntu 20.04

We can install Pixbuf in two ways, and each has its advantages. They are pretty easy to do.

1. **Using the Ubuntu Software Center:** Ubuntu has complete application shops in all of Linux. Pixbuf can be quickly installed on Ubuntu. Open Ubuntu Software Center from the main menu.

2. **Download the software from Package Manager:** This can ensure that you have the most stable version.

On the Ubuntu Software screen, in the search bar, type "pixbuf" and wait. Then choose the correct result.

When you click Pixbuf, you will get information about the package to be installed. Start the installation using the Install button.

Install Pixbuf on Ubuntu Using the Terminal

Some prefer to use the terminal because it is a direct way to install programs. You can install Pixbuf from the terminal using this command:

$ sudo snap install pixbuf-desktop

Enter your password, the installation process begins.
Last, you can launch it from the main system menu.

Running Pixbuf

1. As you run the program starts, you will see a welcome screen.

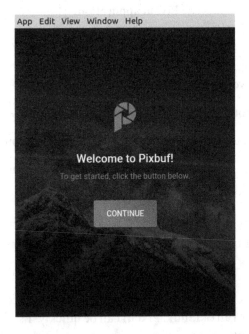

Pixbuf application window.

2. Click on the Continue, and you will see a screen to ask for your email address to create your account.

3. You can create your account via social networks, such as Facebook or Twitter.

4. Next, you enter the user password.

5. You will see a screen for the application when you are done.

6. And close it, the main interface of Pixbuf. Now you can use the application without any problems.

CLEMENTINE MUSIC PLAYER

It is a cross-platform music player and a competitor to Rhythmbox, the default music player on Ubuntu. It is a fast and easy-to-use music player thanks to its user-friendly interface. It supports audio playback in all the major audio file formats.

Apart from music from the local library, you can also listen to online radio from Spotify, Soundcloud, etc. It offers more features like intelligent and dynamic playlists, syncing music from cloud storage drives like Dropbox, Google Drive, etc.

Installing Clementine from the Standard Repository

The Clementine music player is included in Ubuntu 20.04 standard repository and installed with the apt command.

The given command to install Clementine from the standard repository:

$ sudo apt install clementine

Press Y to continue installing Clementine.

Once the Clementine player is installed, verify the installation with the command given below:

$ clementine --version

The output verifies the installation of Clementine's music player on the Ubuntu system.

Installing Clementine via Snap

Snap comes pre-installed on Ubuntu 20.04. Clementine is available from the snap application manager and can be installed using the command:

$ sudo snap install clementine

After the installation, type the command given below to check the installed version:

$ sudo snap info clementine

Installing Clementine from Ubuntu Software Center

It is recommended to install the Clementine music player application using a graphical user interface. Using Ubuntu Software Center, you can install the Clementine by point and click method. Open the Software Center application from the Application menu and search for Clementine.

Clementine music player application.

To install Clementine, click on "Install".

BLENDER APPLICATION

It is free and open-source 3D creation software that you can use to create 3D printed video games, models, animated films, etc., and it comes with an integrated game engine in which you can develop and test video games.

It has an exemplary user interface that is easy to use, and it includes features like a built-in render engine, digital sculpturing, simulation tool, animation tools, and many more. It is the best application you will ever find for Ubuntu, considering its accessibility and the features it offers.

Install Blender on Ubuntu Linux Desktop

In this section, you will learn:

1. How to install Blender from the command line

2. How to install Blender using the graphical user interface

Blender installation on Ubuntu step by step instructions:

Installing Blender from the Command Line

You can start by opening a terminal and execution the bellow apt command:

```
$ sudo snap install Blender --classic
```

You can start the Blender using the below command:

```
$ Blender
```

Install Blender Using the Graphical User Interface

Use the top Activities menu to open the Software application.

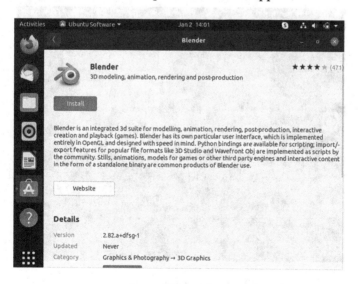

Blender application.

1. Then search for Blender application.

2. To start the installation, press the Install button.

3. Enter your username and password, and the user needs to belong to sudo administrative group.

4. Start the Blender application.

Authentication required.

Blender application window.

AUDACITY APPLICATION

It is an open-source audio application that you can use to record and edit audio files and record audio from various inputs like a microphone, electric guitar, etc. It also allows you to edit and trim audio clips according to your need.

Recently, it has released new features for Ubuntu, including theme improvements, zoom toggle command, etc. Apart from these, it offers various audio effects, including noise reduction and many more.

How to Install Audacity Audio Editor in Ubuntu
New in Audacity:

- It works on Mac Catalina.
- New Multi-View model for tracks.
- Export audio to Opus in Windows, Linux.
- It is easier to convert labels between point labels and range labels.
- New Loudness Normalization effect.
- New RMS measurement analyzer.
- It presets for more effects can be imported and exported.
- New Noise Gate effect.
- New Spectral Delete effect.
- Tons of bug fixes.
- New Time Toolbar.

ow to Install Audacity 2.4.1 in Ubuntu:
The PPA has built the new release for Ubuntu various versions like 20.04, 19.10, 18.04, and 16.04.

1. Open terminal via Ctrl + Alt +T keyboard shortcut or by searching for "terminal" from the Application menu. Open and run the command to add the PPA:

   $ sudo add-apt-repository PPA:ubuntuhandbook1/audacity

Type user password when you enter it prompts and hit to continue button.

2. If you have the last version installed, you can upgrade it via Software Updater after adding the PPA.

or run the following commands to check updates and install audacity:

To update, you can use the below command:

$ sudo apt update

To install, you can use the below command:

$ sudo apt install audacity

- **Uninstall:** Launch the Software & Updates utility and navigate to the "Other Software" to remove the PPA. To remove software, either use package manager or run command in terminal:

sudo apt-get remove --autoremove audacity audacity-data

- **Vim:** Vim is an Integrated Development Environment that can use as a standalone application or command-line interface for programming in various major programming languages like Python.

Most programmers like coding in Vim because it is a fast and highly customizable IDE. Initially, you may find it challenging to use, but you will quickly get used to it.

$ sudo apt-get install vim

INKSCAPE APPLICATION

Inkscape is an open-source, cross-platform graphics editor, which will find similar to Corel Draw and Adobe Illustrator. By using it, you can create and edit vector graphics such as diagrams, charts, logos, illustrations, etc.

Inkscape uses Scalable Vector Graphics and an open XML-based standard as a primary format. It supports various formats, including JPEG, PNG, GIF, PDF, AI, VSD, etc.

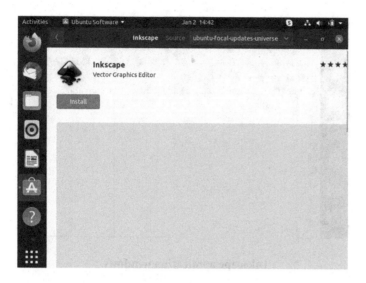

Inkscape application.

Ubuntu carries Inkscape in their primary software sources. To install it, open up Ubuntu software, search "Inkscape", and click the "Install" button. Alternatively, open up a terminal and enter the command below.

$ sudo apt install Inkscape

The Inkscape that Ubuntu carries is modern, but the Inkscape developers have an official PPA that users can enable to get the latest version. Once you enable, the Inkscape on Ubuntu will be more up to date, and to allow the Inkscape PPA, enter the following command given below:

$ sudo add-apt-repository PPA:Inkscape.dev/stable

Using add-apt-repository to add the PPA adds a new software source to the system. To make Ubuntu aware of the recent changes, you will need to run the update command.

$ sudo apt update

Inkscape application windows.

Using update in the latest updates. Given that Ubuntu now uses the new Inkscape PPA, some updates to Inkscape are ready to install. To upgrade Ubuntu to the recent version of Inkscape, you can use the upgrade command.

$ sudo apt upgrade -y

If you want to remove the command to get rid of Inkscape use the below command,

$ sudo apt remove Inkscape

SHOTCUT APPLICATION

It is a free, open-source, cross-platform video editing application developed by Meltytech, LLC on the MLT Multimedia Framework. It is one of the most powerful video editors you will ever find for Linux distros as it supports all the primary audio, video, and image formats.

It gives the ability to edit multiple tracks with various file formats using non-linear video editing. It also comes with support for 4K video resolutions and features like different audio and video filters, tone generator, audio mixing, and many others.

Install Shotcut on Ubuntu Linux

Video editing is straightforward, and you should try Shotcut Video Editor.
How to Install Shotcut on Ubuntu Linux

How to Install Handbrake (Open-Source Video Transcoder) on Ubuntu 20.04 Linux

Video editing is straightforward, and you should try Shotcut Video Editor.
According to the Shotcut website:

- It is a free, open-source, cross-platform video editor.

- Major features include:

- It supports a wide range of formats.

- No import is required, meaning native editing.

- It is black magic Design support for input and preview monitoring.

- It supports resolution to 4k.

In further, it makes support for many audio and video formats one of its main strengths. Created with some of the essential open-source technologies, such as QT and FFmpeg with Shotcut, you will have a professional editor within reach.
Some features of Shotcut are:

- It supports the latest audio and video formats thanks to FFmpeg.

- It supports famous image formats such as BMP, GIF, JPEG, PNG, SVG, TGA, TIFF, WebP, and image sequences.

- There is no need to import – native timeline editing.

- It is frame-accurate, seeking many formats.

- It uses a multi-format timeline: mix and match resolutions and frame rates within a project.

- Ability to capture using webcam.

- Audio scopes: loudness, peak meter, waveform, spectrum analyzer.

- It can control volume.

- Support audio filters.

- It supports cross-platform: available on Windows, Linux, and macOS.

- Codec is independent, so it does not rely on system codecs.

- It can run as a portable app from an external drive.

Install Shotcut on Ubuntu 20.04

Shotcut is software that provides excellent support for Linux and Ubuntu is the most famous distribution. Therefore, there are several ways to perform the installation.

Install Shotcut Using the Ubuntu Software Center

In other words, we have already commented that Ubuntu's application shop is one of the most complete. We can find many different applications to benefit our system in it fully.

So, you can open it from the main menu of Ubuntu.

Then in the search bar, enter Shotcut and get the best result, which is the first one.

When you click on the result, you will see detailed information about the package. Start the installation by clicking on the Install button.

Then you can execute the program from the main menu.

Using the Snap Command

If you prefer to use the terminal, you can use the snap command to perform the installation.

So, open a terminal window from the main menu or press CTRL + ALT + T keys and execute:

```
$ sudo snap install shotcut – classic
```

After entering the correct password, the download and installation process will begin.

You can run the application from the main menu as the previous method.

Using AppImage Format

Another alternative is to use AppImage, which is not an installation, but it is also helpful to have it on Ubuntu.

You can download Shotcut from this link or also use wget in the terminal:

wget https://www.fosshub.com/Shotcut.html?dwl=shotcut-linux-x86
_64-201032.AppImage

Then open the browser and run it by double-clicking. It is simple and works similarly to a portable.

Web Browser

Ubuntu operating system comes with Firefox as the default browser. We can also use more than one web browser to distinguish between different types of works.

1. **Google Chrome:** It is the most used web browser for various reasons. With Google account, it allows you to sync across devices. There are plenty of extensions and apps that enhance its capabilities. You can easily install Chrome on Ubuntu.

2. **Brave:** Google Chrome can be the most used web browser, but it's a privacy invader. An alternative browser is it can block ads and tracking scripts by default. It provides you with a faster and secure web browsing experience.

SAYONARA APPLICATION

It is a mini, lightweight music player with an excellent user interface and comes with all the other essential features you would expect in a standard music player. It integrates nicely with the Ubuntu desktop environment and does not eat up your system RAM.

Points:

- It is the lesser-known music players for Linux that deserve more attention.

- It has a fantastic user interface, and the default dark theme gives it an attractive look.

- It is a tiny music player that has released its first version under GPL 3 open source license.

Sayonara Features

It may be a small application, but it is not negligible on the features side. It packs all the essential features you would expect in a regular music player. Some of the main features are:

- It supports various music and playlist formats.

- It has a media library with a search function.

- It has a directory view.

- It supports external device.

- It has a Genre organization.

- The Playlist view is grouped into tabs.

- It has various views ranging from equalizer to spectrum.

- It has multiple shortcut keys.

- Desktop integration with desktop notification, sound menu integration, and media key integration.

- It has an Album art.

- It has an internet stream with services like SoundCloud and Last.fm.

- It supports podcasts and internet radio.

- It supports several languages other than English.

- It has a built-in option to record streaming music.

How to Install Sayonara Music Player

It is available for Linux and supports all major Linux platforms, including Mageia Linux.

Let us look at how to install Sayonara audio player in Ubuntu Linux distributions. Various deb packages are available that you can easily download and install by double-clicking on them.

Alternatively, if you like to use PPA, you can use the official PPA site to install it. The PPA is available for Ubuntu OS and the above versions. So it won't work with the Mint 17 series.

$ sudo apt-add-repository PPA:lucioc/sayonara

$ sudo apt-get update

$ sudo apt-get install sayonara

If you want to uninstall the installed Sayonara package by PPA

Fedora users can install Sayonara using the command given below

$ sudo dnf install sayonara

Experiencing Sayonara Music Player

We had a quick test run of the Sayonara audio player. It claims to be a lightweight application.

Sayonara Music Player

- **Easy on resources:** You can notice that it is well integrated with the desktop. You might have desktop notifications for track changes. You can change the tracks, pause the music with the media key on my XPS 13 laptop.

- **Sayonara music player desktop integration:** Sayonara is automatically added to the system tray icon, giving you quick access to the player in the top or bottom panel.

- **Sayonara music player for Linux:** It is added to the sound menu for quick access.

- **Using Sayonara music player:** The feature of adding tracks to the current playlist is confusing. But double-clicking on a track does not start to play but adds it to the current playing list.

Sayonara Application.

MUSICBRAINZ APPLICATION

MusicBrainz Picard is a cross-platform music application that runs on Linux, Mac OS X, and Windows which allows you to clean your local music by automatically updating the artist, album, track information, and album art cover for the per song.

MusicBrainz itself is a massive open-source database of music.

It is a tool that uses the database to identify and tag your music and checks the songs in the MusicBrainz database to see if it can find a match. If it can't find a match, it uses AcoustIDto figure out the song. It supports many audio file formats, can use audio fingerprints, performs CD look-ups, and supports Unicode.

FEATURES

Picard comes with new changes, with the significant difference being a switch in the dependencies. The latest version has been ported to Python 3, 5, or PyQt 5.7. It now also includes HiDPI and Retina support and also many bug fixes. It helps you organize your music collection by renaming your music files and sorting them into a folder structure exactly how you want it. Various plug-ins and you can even write you are own available.

Some of the significant changes and bug fixes that can be seen in MusicBrainz Picard 2.0 include:

- Now, it supports tagging DSF file.

- Picard 2.0 supports only 64 bit.

- A keyboard shortcut adds for deleting scripts from options > scripting page.

- Provides improvements to user interface.

- It can be fixed saving tags for files on NAS devices.

- It can automatically overwrite existing cover art that has been fixed.

- It makes multi-value script functions now work well.

- It is incompatible plug-ins can be loaded with Picard 2.0.

- Support for HiDPI and Retina.

- It crashes when using the edit tag dialogue has been fixed.

- Its search crashes due to AttributeError has been fixed.

- Now, the file can be opened in WAV.

- It supports all music formats, including MP3, FLAC, OGG, M4A, WMA, WAV, and more.

- It uses AcoustID audio fingerprints, allowing files to be identified by the actual music, even if they have no metadata.

- It uses the open and community-maintained MusicBrainz database to provide information about millions of music releases.

- It can look up entire music CDs with a click.

- If you need any specific feature, you can choose from a selection of available plug-ins or write your own.

- A flexible but easy-to-learn scripting language allows you to specify.

- It can find and download the correct cover art for your albums.

- It is licensed under the General Public License 2.0 or later and is hosted on GitHub, where some awesome developers actively develop it.

HOW TO INSTALL MUSICBRAINZ PICARD IN UBUNTU

The official PPA has built the tagger for Ubuntu 18.04, 18.10.

Launch terminal via Ctrl + Alt + T keyboard shortcut or search for "terminal" from software launcher. When you open it, run the following command to add the PPA:

sudo add-apt-repository PPA:MusicBrainz-developers/stable

Please enter your user password when it prompts and hit Enter to continue.

If the last version was installed, upgrade the software using the Software Updater or run the following commands in the terminal to install or upgrade to MusicBrainz Picard 2.0:

$ sudo apt-get update

$ sudo apt-get install Picard

MusicBrainz application.

Uninstall

Launch Software & Updates and navigate to the Another Software tab to remove the PPA.

To remove MusicBrainz Picard music tagger, run the below command in terminal:

sudo apt-get remove --autoremove Picard

KRITA APPLICATION

It is a free and open-source digital painting application, and you can create digital art, comics, and animation with it. It is professional-grade software and is even used as the primary software in art schools.

It is mainly built for KDE Plasma. It has versions for Windows and macOS, making it a cross-platform software and fully-featured digital art studio that offers users many powerful features despite a minimalist UI. It has features like an advanced brush engine, non-destructive layers and masks, support for numerous image formats and color patterns, and more.

Painting applications are not similar to image editors though their functionalities overlap. Here are some paint apps you can use in Ubuntu.

Installing Krita

Ubuntu offers various ways for users to install Krita on their computers. The following sections will take a look at some of these installation methods.

Installing Krita with a Snap

A straightforward way of installing Krita on your system is by using a Snap. Snaps are packages recently developed by Canonical that allows users to install an application on any distribution of Linux without undergoing an error due to the software not being supported.

To install Krita using the snap, open the terminal by clicking Ctrl + Alt + T or searching in the Dash. Then, enter the following command:

```
$ sudo snap install Krita
```

Installing Krita with the PPA Repository

Because Snaps are still not stable, many users still opt to install PPA repositories applications. To install Krita using your PPA repository, you will first need to add Krita to your system, which can be got by running the following command:

```
$ sudo add-apt-repository PPA:kritalime/PPA
```

Then, the command to update the system by running the command below:

```
$ sudo apt update
```

Finally, enter the next command to install Krita onto your Ubuntu system:

$ sudo apt-get install Krita

Once you get your Krita application, double-click to open it and you will get a window like the one given below.

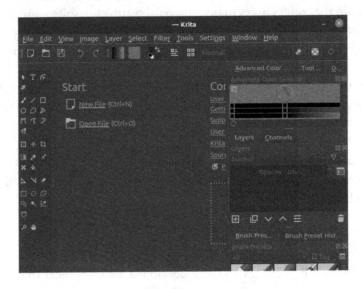

Kirta application window.

PINTA APPLICATION

It is a free drawing application that is quite popular among Linux users. It is available for all Linux, Windows, and Mac OS X platforms.

While GIMP is popular as a full-featured image editing software, Pinta is a paint and drawing tool.

New Features in Pinta

In 2022, Pinta released version 2.0, fixing over 50 bugs and introducing new features. New features are as follows:

- Line tool now supports drawing curves and arrows.

- The given shapes can be edited even after being drawn.

- Now, all shape tools help draw dashed lines.

- All selection tools now help the Union, Exclude, Xor, and It supports Intersection modes.

- Add-in manager currently consists of add-ins.

- New options in command-line usage.

Install Pinta in Ubuntu

It is more like Paint and with your painting made simple.

Pinta can also be installed using the Software Center, and below the approach is the command line.

Install PPA

$ sudo add-apt-repository PPA:pinta-maintainers/pinta-stable

Update System with Package List

You can upgrade Pinta from an old release via Software Updater (Update Manager):

$ sudo apt-get update

Install and Remove Pinta

Run apt command in terminal to install or upgrade the software:

$ sudo apt-get install pinta

And to remove Pinta via command run the following command:

$ sudo apt remove --autoremove pinta

Once you get your Pinta Application, double-click to open it and you will get a window like the one given below.

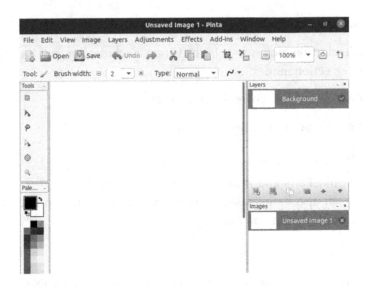

Pinta application window.

TELEGRAM APPLICATION

It is a cloud-based messaging and VoIP platform that has had a lot of popularity in these years. It is a free open-source and cross-platform messenger where you can send messages, share photos, videos, audio, and other various files like documents, your live location.

Telegram features are secreting chats, voice messages, bots, and telescopes for video messages, live locations, and social login. Privacy and security are prioritized in Telegram, so all messages you send and receive are end-to-end encrypted.

It is available for GNU/Linux, Windows, macOS, Android, iOS, and Windows Phone. We will show you two ways to install Telegram on Ubuntu.

Telegram Features

1. It syncs messages across any device, computer, tablet, or smartphone.

2. It is an unlimited file sharing with up to 2 GB per file. Send messages, photos, videos, and any file.

3. It can secure your chat with end-to-end encryption.

4. It can secure and fast video calls, which supports picture-in-picture mode.

5. You can switch video on or off at any time during voice calls.

6. You can also create groups of up to 200,000 people.

7. You can create channels for broadcasting to an unlimited audience and upload a video to your profile.

8. Multi-accounts. Stay signed in on all three accounts from different phone numbers without logging out.

9. And more.

Way to Install Telegram

1. Install Telegram on Ubuntu using Snap

Canonical has packaged a Telegram snap app. You can find it in Ubuntu Software by searching for "telegram" in the search bar. Now, click the install button to install it on Ubuntu.

You can open a terminal window and enter the following command to find the name of the Telegram snap package.

snap find | grep Telegram

Then run this command to install it:

sudo snap install telegram-desktop

Install Telegram on Ubuntu via PPA

There is also a Telegram PPA available for Ubuntu. Run the following three commands to install from PPA:

sudo add-apt-repository PPA:atareao/telegram

$ sudo apt-get update

$ sudo apt-get install telegram

Once you get your Telegram Application, double-click to open it and you will get a window like the one given below.

Telegram application window.

PPA or Snap?

The Telegram snap app is that there is no tray icon. In addition, it cannot open the link via web browsers, and CJK fonts are not displayed correctly.

A snap package is good to use because a sandbox confines it. The default display server on the Ubuntu desktop is still X11, where X11 is inherently insecure. Applications in it can steal other applications' data.

Install Telegram from the Software Repository

Telegram is included in the default Ubuntu repository. You can easily install it using the following command:

```
$ sudo apt install telegram-desktop
```

Screenshot and screen recording tools in Ubuntu

SHUTTER APPLICATION

Shutter is a tool for taking screenshots. You can do quick editing to those screenshots, like adding arrows, text, or resizing the images—one of the best apps for Ubuntu.

Install Shutter Screenshot Tool in Ubuntu

It is a neat tool for adding arrows and text to the images. You can use it to resize Ubuntu images or whatever Linux distribution you are using. Most of the screenshot tutorials on its FOSS have been edited on Shutter.

Here we are using the concept of PPA. If not, I highly recommend reading the detailed guide given below to know more about PPA and how to use it.

What Is a PPA?

PPA stands for "Personal Package Archive" and is an application repository used to upgrade and install packages from unofficial sources.

Difference between PPAs and Other Repositories

DEB packages can be served through any repository that adheres to Debian's rules and guidelines for creating and maintaining repositories. For example, the OpenSUSE build service provides repositories used to install and upgrade packages in Ubuntu.

On the other side, a PPA is hosted on Canonical servers and is served through its Launchpad platform. Users hosting PPAs on Launchpad do not require their server to distribute packages, while other repositories need a server to do the same.

Open a terminal window and run the given command to add the new repository

```
$ sudo add-apt-repository -y PPA:linuxuprising/shutter
```

There is no need to use apt update anymore because starting Ubuntu 18.04, the repositories are updated automatically.

Now you can use the apt command to install Shutter

```
$ sudo apt install shutter
```

Removing Shutter installed via PPA

To remove Shutter from your system, execute the following code

```
$ sudo apt remove shutter
```

Following, remove the PPA from your list of repositories

sudo add-apt-repository --remove PPA:linuxuprising/shutter

KAZAM SCREEN CASTER APPLICATION

For screencasting in Ubuntu Linux, you can use FFmpeg in the terminal or graphical tools like Kazam screen caster. Kazam is an open-source and feature-rich visual screen recorder for Linux.

Features of Kazam

- It can capture the contents of the current screen.

- It can capture the contents of all of your screens.

- It can capture contents of a single window such as a terminal window.

- It can capture a pre-selected area of your screen.

- You have an option to record sound from a speaker or microphone so that you can add background music or your commentary when doing screencasting.

- It also can take a screenshot of your screen, window, or pre-selected area.

Install Kazam Screen Caster on Ubuntu

Kazam Screencaster is available from the Ubuntu repository; run the below command in the terminal:

$ sudo apt install Kazam

If VLC cannot play the saved video recording, you can try the Totem video player, which can be installed with:

$ sudo apt install totem

Keyboard Shortcuts Kazam Screencaster

- **SUPER-CTRL-Q**: Quit

- **SUPER-CTRL-W**: Show/Hide the main window

- **SUPER-CTRL-R**: Start Recording

- **SUPER-CTRL-F**: Finish Recording

KazamCaster application window.

MAILSPRING

Mailspring is also known as Nylas Mail or Nylas N1. It is an open-source email client and saves all the emails locally on the computer to access them anytime you need.

It has features of advanced search using AND and OR. These operations allow you to search for emails based on different parameters.

It comes with a fantastic user interface which you will find only on a handful of other mail clients. Some of the features of Mailspring offer privacy and security, scheduler, contact manager, calendar, and more.

Install and Use Mailspring on Ubuntu

1. Installing Mailspring using Snap

It can be easy to install by using a Snap. Snaps are compressed forms of applications that contain all the dependencies inside them. They are various advantages of installing because you can install it with a single command, and these run in any Linux distribution. Install it using Snapcraft, run the following command into the terminal:

$ sudo snap install mainspring

To uninstall using mainspring using SNAP

$ sudo snap remove mainspring

Download Mailspring Using DEB Packages

Run the command in the terminal to download the latest version of the Mailspring.

$ sudo apt install wget -y

wget https://updates.getmailspring.com/download?platform=linuxDeb -O mailspring.deb

Using Mailspring on Ubuntu Software

After installing Mailspring using Software, you can find it in the list of your installed applications.

Uninstall Mailspring

You can uninstall using the following commands:

$ sudo apt remove mainspring

$ sudo apt autoremove

Open it up; you will see the following screen appear and click on Get Started to move ahead.

Mailspring application window.

DROPBOX APPLICATION

It is a cloud storage platform, and its Linux clients work well on Ubuntu. While Google Drive comes on Ubuntu 16.04 LTS and later, Dropbox is still the best cloud storage tool on Linux in terms of features it offers.

Install Dropbox on Ubuntu Desktop

Get Dropbox installer for Ubuntu. Ubuntu offers DEB files for Dropbox installer. Go to the download portion of the website, https://www.dropbox.com/install-linux.

Install Dropbox Installer

The deb file downloaded is an installer for Dropbox. Actual Dropbox installation starts later. To install the deb file, double-click on it, select Open with Software option, and Install.

It opens the Software Center, and you can click the Install button.

Start Dropbox Installation

Dropbox installer is now installed. Press the Windows key and search for Dropbox and click on it. The first launch shows two popups—one about restarting Nautilus and the other about Dropbox installation. Once Dropbox is installed, it takes to the Dropbox login page automatically.

Once you sign in, you will see a Dropbox folder created in your home directory, and your files from the cloud start appearing here.

FOLIATE – PUB READER APPLICATION

The Foliate is GTK-based boasts a clean and clutter-free UI.

It provides a stack of font sizing, spacing, and page layout options, supports text notes, dictionary lookups, bookmarks, and tracks your page progress.

Foliate is accessible and is available from Flathub and the Snap Store. A standard installer package is also available from GitHub, linked below.

Enable Snap

If you're running Ubuntu 16.04 LTS (Xenial Xerus) or later, including Ubuntu 18.04 LTS (Bionic Beaver) and Ubuntu 20.04 LTS, you don't need to do anything.

For versions of Ubuntu between 14.04 LTS and 15.10 and Ubuntu flavors that don't include snap by default, a snap can be installed from the Ubuntu Software Center by searching for snaps.

Alternatively, a snap can be installed from the command line

$ sudo apt update

$ sudo apt install snap

Install Foliate

To install Foliate, use the following command:

$ sudo snap install foliate

Once you get your Foliate Application, double-clicking to open it, you will get a window like the one given below.

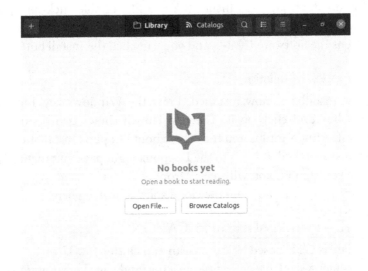

Foliate application window.

TILIX TERMINAL EMULATOR

It is an emulator that helps interact with the computer machine and perform operations using commands. It is a tiling terminal emulator known as Terminix, and it is an enhancement over a common terminal and provides some primary features.

- It enable users to split the terminal into different sections in order to avoid switching between multiple tabs of the terminal.

- It allows arranging and rearranging the split panes easily using drag and drop.

- Support different terminal themes and layouts.

- It supports notification when the processes are completed.

- It enables to use a transparent background.

- It allows using a keyboard shortcut to show or hide the terminal window.

- It is the highly configurable user interface, background images, etc.

- Input can be synchronized between terminals so commands typed in one terminal are replicated to the others.

Installation in Ubuntu

There are two ways with two methods:

1. Using command.

2. Using Package Manager.

Open terminal and type the command:

$ sudo apt update

$ sudo apt-get install tilix

Installation in Linux

Tilix is generally present in the Arch Linux repository and can be installed with:

$ Pacman -S tilix

Tilix allows tile multiple terminal sessions inside a single unified window horizontally and vertically. It also supports custom titles, custom links, and custom backgrounds. Its feature set comprises drag and drops rearranging, supporting persistent layouts.

ARORA APPLICATION

Benjamin C. Meyer developed the Arora web browser, and it is popular among Linux users for its lightweight nature and flexibility.

Arora is a cross-platform lightweight web browser based on Webkit technology that has been developed by Qt toolkit. The Arora browser has features like the ClicktoFlash plug-in, privacy mode, session management, smart location bar, etc. This tutorial covers the installation procedure of Arora on Linux mint 18.03.

It is a free and open-source web browser that offers features like a dedicated download manager, bookmarks, privacy mode, and tabbed browsing.

Quick Install Steps

1. Run the flag command to install the packages and dependencies quickly:

   $ sudo apt-get update -y.

2. Run the flag command to quickly install the packages and dependencies:

   $ sudo apt-get install -y arora.

3. Now, check the system logs to confirm that there are no errors. You can use ZoomAdmin to review the records, manage servers, host multiple websites and apps on your servers, and more. The apps run in docker containers.

It's an excellent lightweight application with various features like book-marking websites, setting internet proxy addresses if you are working on a proxy-based environment, fast internet website browsing, consuming less memory, downloading manager, Adblocker, etc. Arora browser is not an advanced browser like Google Chrome or Mozilla Firefox, but this application is best for you if you are looking for a simple web browser with standard browsing features. A cross-platform application is available for major operating systems, i.e., Linux, Microsoft Windows, and macOS.

The disadvantages of the Arora web browser are that it's not been updated for the last seven years. The latest update of the application was released in 2010, and also there are no plug-ins and fixes available for Arora browser. Initially, this application was developed by Benjamin C. Meyer using C++ programming language and released under GNU GPL license.

MUMBLE APPLICATION

It is a free, open-source Voice Over IP application designed primarily to be used by gamers. Mumble is similar to TeamSpeak and Ventrilo. Mumble uses a client-server architecture that allows users to talk when connected to the same server. It also has a simple administration interface and features low-latency, high-quality codecs. Murmur allows you to run your own private or public voice chat server for the Mumble client.

Requirements

- 512 MB Droplet
- Ubuntu 14.04

Installation and Launching Mumble

- Installing software using the UI is very simple. On the Ubuntu Activities toolbar, click the Ubuntu Software icon.
- Click on the search and type Mumble in the search bar in the following view.
- All these releases are from different developers. You can click on any to see the developer/source. We prefer the one available from the Ubuntu Bionic Universe

Once you get your Mumble application, double-click to open it and you will get a window like the one given below.

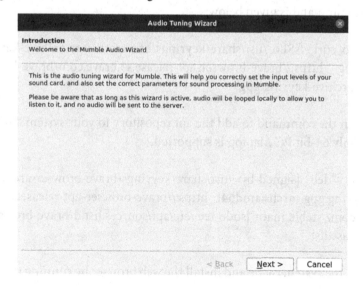

Mumble application window.

BRAVE APPLICATION

It is a free and open-source web browser based on Chromium that blocks ads and trackers so that you can browse any content fast and safely. It does is that it pays to websites and You Tubers on behalf of you. If you prefer contributing to websites and YouTubers rather than seeing advertisements, then this browser is for you. It features a faster page loading speed and blocks ads and trackers by default.

The browser offers an official apt repository. So Ubuntu, Debian, and Linux Mint-based systems can easily install the software and receive updates via built-in update manager utility.

It is a new concept and could be a good browser for those who prefer safe browsing without compromising essential data on the internet.

Firstly, open "terminal" from your system from the start menu. When it opens, paste the command below into the terminal and hit Enter:

```
$ sudo apt install apt-transport-HTTP curl
```

All the necessary packages will start downloading.

Next is to copy and paste the command, run it to download and install the GPG key:

The command is given below:

```
"sudo curl -fsSLo /usr/share/keyrings/brave-browser-archive-keyring.
    gpg  https://brave-browser-apt-release.s3.brave.com/brave-browser
    -archive-keyring.gpg"
```

And run the command to add the apt repository to your system. So far, it is for only 64-bit PC / laptop is supported.

```
echo  "deb  [signed-by=/usr/share/keyrings/brave-browser-archive-ke
    yring.gpg  arch=amd64]  https://brave-browser-apt-release.s3.brave
    .com/ stable main"|sudo tee /etc/apt/sources.list.d/brave-browser-re
    lease.list
```

Refresh the system cache and install the web browser by running the commands as follows:

```
$ sudo apt update
```

```
$ sudo apt install brave-browser
```

To uninstall Brave and its APT repository:

Run the following command in the terminal to remove the Brave web browser

```
$ sudo apt remove --autoremove brave-browser
```

Unlike PPA, Brave apt repository does not list in Software & Updates utility under the Another Software tab. Hence, you can remove the config file easily by running the command in the terminal:

```
$ sudo rm /etc/apt/sources.list.d/brave-browser-release.list
```

SPEEDY DUPLICATE FINDER APPLICATION

The Speedy Duplicate Finder is a cross-platform file finder application that helps you find duplicate files on your system and free up disk space. It is an intelligent tool that searches for duplicate files on the entire hard disk and features a smart filter that helps you find files by file type, extension, or size.

It has a clean and straightforward user interface that is very easy to handle. You can also download it from Software Center, and you can go with disk space clean-up.

Install Speedy Duplicate Finder on Ubuntu 20.04

First, before installing any package on your Ubuntu system server, we always recommend ensuring that all system packages are updated to date.

You can use the following commands to update and upgrade your package

```
$ sudo apt update
```

```
$ sudo apt upgrade
```

Install Speedy Duplicate Finder on Ubuntu System
Using Snap Store for Your Ubuntu System

```
$ sudo apt update
```

```
$ sudo apt install snapd
```

You can install the Speedy Duplicate Finder on your system via the Snap daemon by running the following command below:

```
$ sudo snap install speedy-duplicate-finder
```

Features

- **Blazingly fast**: You can scan 1000 files takes less than a second.

- **Disk support**: You can search for duplicates in folders and on the entire disk.

- **Multiple folders**: You can find duplicates in many folders simultaneously.

- **Intuitively simple**: It is so simple for all ages and all users.

- **Smart filters**: You can easily filter group of duplicates by kind, by extension, or by size.

- **Truly versatile**: It supports major desktop platforms such as Windows, macOS, and Linux.

- **Get and go**: It doesn't require any installation! Good to go as soon as downloaded.

Once you get your Speedy Duplicate Finder application, double-click to open it and you will get a window like the one given below.

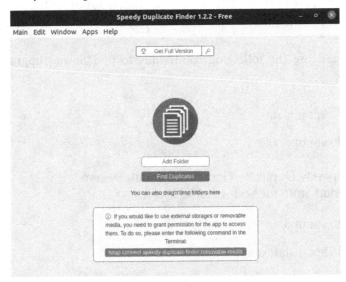

Speedy Duplicate Finder application.

GUAKE APPLICATION

It is a perfect drop-down terminal for GNOME Desktop Environment. Whenever you need it, it comes in a flash and disappears when your task is completed. You need to click the F12 button to launch or exit it, so launching Guake is way faster than launching a new Terminal window.

It is a feature-rich terminal with various features like support for multiple tabs, the ability to save your terminal content to file in a few clicks, and a fully customizable user interface.

Features

- It is a lightweight terminal.

- It is simple easy and elegant.

- It has smooth integration of terminal into GUI.

- It appears when you invoke and disappears once when you are done by pressing a hotkey (F12 by default).

- It supports the Compiz transparency.

- It supports multi-tab and plenty of color palettes.

- You can quick Open in your favorite text editor with a click on a file name.

- It also has customizable hotkeys for tab access, reorganization, background transparency, font size.

- It can be extremely configurable.

- It configures Guake startup by running a bash script when Guake starts.

- Multi-monitor support such as open on a specified monitor, open on mouse monitor.

- It saves terminal content to file.

- It can open URL to your browser.

Installing Guake

To install Guake terminal, use the following command given below:

```
$ sudo apt-get install guake
```

To open guake, execute the following command:

$ guake

After starting it, press F12 (default) to roll down and roll up the terminal on GNOME Desktop. The output of guake is given below.

To run Guake Preferences by running it from Application Menu or by running the below command:

$ guake –preferences

A Guake preference has various tabs such as General, Shell, Scrolling, Appearance, Quick-Open, Keyboard Shortcuts, and Compatibility.

Once you get your Guake Application, double-clicking to open it, you will get a window like the one given below.

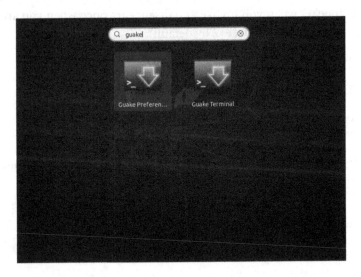

Guake application window.

KDE CONNECT APPLICATION

It is an excellent application on Ubuntu, and you should have loved to list this application much higher in this marathon article, but the competition is intense. KDE Connect helps you get Android smartphone notifications directly on the Ubuntu desktop.

With KDE Connect, you can do a whole lot of other things like check the battery of your phone level, exchange files between computer and

Android phone, clipboard sync, send SMS, and you can use any mobile as a wireless mouse or keyboard.

The application has the best features like receiving phone notifications on your desktop screen to which you can reply, controlling your desktop by making your phone act as a remote control, sharing files between the connected devices, and finding the phone by giving it a ring.

It performs all these functions while keeping a secure protocol on the network to prevent any privacy issues. This application is entirely free and open-source. Having all these features combined inside a single application is quite a feat and makes an excellent application to use.

Installing KDE Connect on Ubuntu

First, you need to install KDE Connect on your system. You can find the KDE Connect package in the official repository of the Linux system. In Ubuntu, the app is supported by its official repository or by installing KDE Connect through the apt command.

Before installing the KDE Connect, your apt-cache of the system must be updated so that there will be no issues later on in the process. To do this, open the terminal window using the shortcut Ctrl + Alt + T, and execute the following command:

```
$ sudo apt-get update
```

Enter the following command to install KDE Connect:

```
$ sudo apt install kdeconnect
```

Installing KDE Connect on Your Android Phone

To connect your mobile with your Ubuntu system, you also need to install the KDE Connect application on the same device. KDE Connect can get both the Google Play Store and F-Droid so that you can install the application from either of these locations.

Setting Up KDE Connect

To use KDE Connect, open the application on your Ubuntu system and Android device. When you click on these items, the application will ask you whether you want to pair your device with the other. Then click request pairing to pair. Once done, your devices should be paired.

It is an open-source emulator which is programmed and developed in Java. It is a cross-platform emulator that lets you access numerous terminals in a single window.

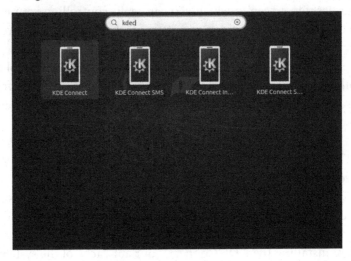

KDE Connect application.

TERMINATOR APPLICATION

A terminal is a must-have tool for system administrators. It provides a command-line interface where most system administration tasks are carried out. Typically, every Linux distribution provides a terminal to launch and run commands.

However, the default terminal with most distributions is basic and uninteresting. And this is where Terminator comes in. Written in Java, Terminator is a free and open-source terminal emulator written in Java. It is cross-platform that can run on Linux, macOS, UNIX, and even available on Microsoft Windows.

Terminator provides additional features to enhance your productivity. For example, you can split your terminal either vertically or horizontally such that you have two or more shell workspaces on the same window. In addition, you get special key bindings that help you seamlessly switch or navigate between the workspaces.

Update Packages

We will update the package lists on our Ubuntu 20.04 system to get started. Here, I'm using Ubuntu 20.04 MATE edition.

$ sudo apt update

Once the update completes, follow that the next step.

Install Terminator

The terminator package is available on the Official Ubuntu repository. Therefore, you can easily install it using the APT package manager as indicated.

$ sudo apt install terminator

The command downloads the Terminator package from the repository and installs it on your system.

Launching and Using Terminator

When Terminator installed, use the application menu to search it and launch it. In the standard GNOME environment, click on Activities at the far left corner and type "Terminator" to explore it. To launch Terminator, click on the Terminator icon.

The terminal window can split into two with one workspace above the other.

Once you get your Font Manager application, double-clicking to open it, you will get a window like the one given below.

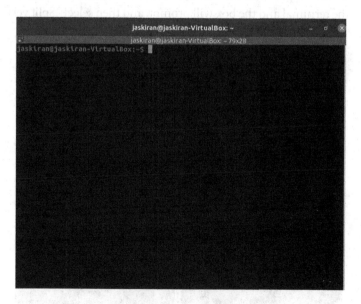

Terminator application window.

You can use a split-screen terminal within the same window stacked over another terminal. To perform this, right-click anywhere within the terminal and the box will prompt, and then select "Split horizontally".

Terminator splitting horizontally window.

You can use a split-screen in vertical. To perform this, right-click anywhere within the terminal and the box will prompt, and then select "Split vertically".

Terminator splitting vertically window.

Terminator can split-screen into both horizontally or vertically once.

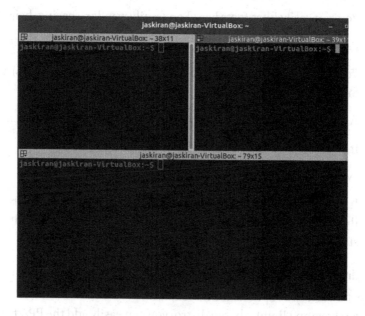

Terminator can split-screen into both horizontally or vertically once

FONT MANAGER APPLICATION

It is a lightweight tool for managing, adding, removing fonts on your Ubuntu system. It is specially built for the GNOME desktop environment, and users who don't know how to handle fonts using the command line will find this tool very useful.

Font Manager is a dedicated application to help you manage fonts and get the details of the font family, variations available, and can filter, tweak based on their height, width, spacing, and more. Assuming it is a simple app, you do not find many features, but I'll briefly highlight a few things below.

Gtk+ Font Manager is not meant to be for professional users, and it has a simple user interface that you will find very easy to navigate. You need to download font files from the internet and add them using Font Manager.

Features of Font Manager

- Font Manager Settings
- It can add fonts

- It can remove fonts

- You can easily filter fonts based on family, vendor, spacing, height, etc.

- Perform tweak the scaling factor of fonts

- You can easily adjust the anti-aliasing (softness/sharpness) of the font

- Also, can add font sources to preview them before installing it

- It offers keyboard shortcuts to manage things quickly

- available Google fonts integration out-of-the-box

- It gives detailed information on characters available in the family font, license, font size, vendor, file type, spacing, width, and style.

Installing Font Manager on Linux

You get a variety of options for installation.

If you have an Ubuntu-based distro, you can easily add the PPA through the commands below to install font manager:

$ sudo add-apt-repository PPA:font-manager/staging

$ sudo apt update

$ sudo apt install font-manager

You need to enable Flatpak on your Ubuntu system and then search on your software center (if supports Flatpak integration) or type in the following command to install it:

$ flatpak install flathub org.gnome.FontManagers

Once you get your Font Manager Application, double-clicking to open it, you will get a window like the one given below.

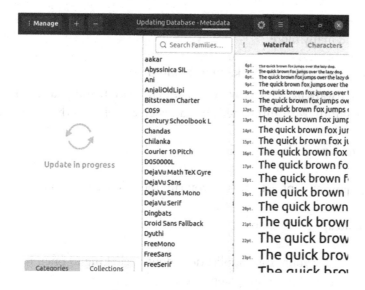

Font Manager application window.

APRIL DOCUMENT VIEWER APPLICATION

It is a simple document viewer which supports file formats like Portable Document Format (PDF), PostScript (PS), Encapsulated PostScript (EPS), DJVU, and DVI. April comes bundled with the MATE desktop environment, and it is identical to Evince, which is the default document on most Linux distros.

It has a lightweight and straightforward user interface which is highly customizable and offers features like search, bookmarks, and UI includes thumbnails on the left-hand side.

It's an excellent lightweight MATE desktop environment application that comes with various features mentioned below:

- It supports different documents, i.e., PDF, XPS, DJVU, CBR Comics, and many more.

- You can use the document viewer Linux application to print documents.

- You can also find more basic features in the application like copy texts, bookmark pages, highlight texts, search for any reader.

- You can use shortcuts (keyboard) to copy, paste, add bookmarks, and many more.

Install April Software Package in Ubuntu

April software package provides document viewer, and you can install in your Ubuntu by running the commands given below in the terminal:

$ sudo apt-get install atril

To update your apt-get package you run the below command:

$ sudo apt-get update

Once you get your April application, double-clicking to open it, you will get a window like the one given below.

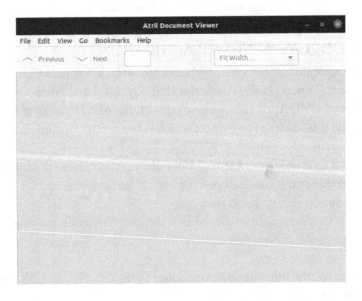

April application window.

NOTEPADQQ APPLICATION

Suppose you have ever worked on Notepad++ in Windows and looked for a similar Linux program. It is a simple, powerful text editor which you can use for daily tasks or programming in various languages.

Notepad++ is the commonly used text editor or source code editor in Microsoft Windows. In Ubuntu, "notepadqq" is the alternate of Notepad++. We can say that notepadqq is Notepad++ for Ubuntu Linux. It is the open-source text editor or code editor developed for developers.

Besides a simple text editor, it has some fantastic features. You can set a theme between dark and light color schemes, multiple selection, regular expression search, and real-time highlighting.

Some of the features of Notepadqq are listed below:

- Syntax highlighter for 100+ languages

- Use of color scheme

- Multiple selections

- Use of regular expression search

- Code folding

- Comment and display mathematical formulas

Installation Steps of Notepadqq on Ubuntu

Add Ubuntu PPA Repository

Note that the "notepadqq" package is not available in the default Ubuntu repository, so we must add the Notepaddqq PPA repository using the below command.

$ sudo add-apt-repository PPA:notepadqq-team/notepadqq

Refresh the Repositories using the below apt-get command.

$ sudo apt-get update

or

$ sudo apt update

Install Notepaddqq Debian Package

Now you can install the notepadqq package from the command line using the following apt-get command,

$ sudo apt-get install notepadqq -y

or

$ sudo apt install notepadqq –y

Once you get your Notepadqq Application, double-clicking to open it, you will get a window like the one given below.

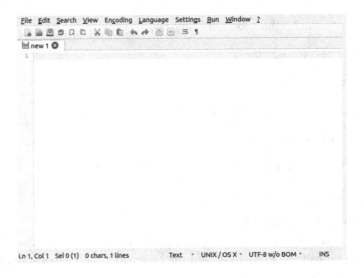

Notepadqq application window.

We are installing notepadqq via Ubuntu Software app

Search for the dash, access Ubuntu Software and in the app, search "notepadqq", then click on Search and then click on Install.

Then we click on Install, it prompts the password, type the password, and click on Authenticate.

When the installation is complete, you have the following screen. From there, we can start accessing it by clicking on "Launch".

MYPAINT APPLICATION

It is a free and open-source graphics editor that focuses on digital painting rather than image manipulation and post-processing. It is a cross-platform application and is more or less similar to Corel Painter.

MyPaint could be an excellent alternative to those who use the Microsoft Paint application on Windows. It has a primary user interface that is fast and powerful. MyPaint is available in Software Center for download.

MyPaint is an open-source, fast, free raster, easy-to-use painting software similar to the other Corel painter. Some graphics editors or digital painters use this app to do different projects and are compatible with all OS such as Windows, macOS, Mac OS X, and UNIX-like.

The developers are regularly working to remove fixes bugs or deliver the best possible experience to a user. So, if you are a Linux-UNIX user and want to install MyPaint, follow the given details. You will get brief information on the installation of MyPaint on Ubuntu.

Some Features of MyPaint

- It has a simple user interface with layer management and symmetry modes.

- It has sensitive graphics tablet support, Python 3 support, and a dynamic brush library designed to integrate into different platforms.

- The canvas does not require predetermination of image size.

There are three ways to download and install.

1. **Install MyPaint Using Terminal**: First, open the terminal window by pressing CTRL + ALT + T buttons altogether, then execute the below command:

   $ sudo apt update -y

   To install it, enter the given command in the terminal:

   $ sudo apt-get install -y mypaint

2. **Install MyPaint Using Flathub**: Before going forward, we have to set up "Flathub" in the system to install it easily. So now, execute the following command as given below:

   $ flatpak install flathub org.MyPaint.MyPaint

To launch the MyPaint, use the following command in the terminal window:

$ flatpak run org.MyPaint.MyPaint

3. **Install MyPaint Using AppImage**: First, download the MyPaint application from the page and execute the below command.

(You can get your Mypaint AppImage from this Github link: https://github.com/AppImage/appimaged)
For example:

$ wget Paste_Your_Github_link_here

It gives permission for executions to run the MyPaint system using the chmod command:

$ chmod 755 MyPaint-v2.0.1.AppImage

How to Remove MyPaint on Ubuntu

We can easily remove or uninstall the MyPaint package from the Ubuntu system. To remove the application of MyPaint, run the command in the terminal given below:

$ sudo apt-get remove mypaint

If you can also remove MyPaint along with its packages to do the same, then run the following command:

$ sudo apt-get remove --auto-remove mypaint

Once you get your MyPaint application, double-clicking to open it, you will get a window like the one given below.

MyPaint application window.

Uninstall MyPaint Using Purging

Suppose you use MyPaint with the purge package and remove all the configuration and dependent packages. In this case, we have to run the following commands:

$ sudo apt-get purge --auto-remove mypaint

$ sudo apt-get purge mypaint

The packages all get removed when you use the purge option with autoremove.

CHAPTER SUMMARY

In this chapter, you received lots of application that you can install in your Ubuntu system using command line or by other Ubuntu built-in software application.

CHAPTER 5

Ubuntu Commands

IN THIS CHAPTER

> ➢ Introduction to CLI

> ➢ Basic commands

The previous chapter was about the Ubuntu application. Ubuntu supports so many applications that you can install them using the command line or the Ubuntu software, which is a built-in application.

This chapter discusses the commands used to control the Ubuntu interface and commands that can do various operations like moving you to other paths using the cd command. You can easily list all the files and folders using ls, create files and folders using mkdir, and touch. We will discuss each of them with an example.

INTRODUCTION

Many essential tasks in Linux we do are from both graphical interfaces and commands. However, the command line has always been the interface of choice for Linux power users. With computer experience, you can probably figure out, for example, how to add a user, change the time and date, and configure a printer from a GUI. However, you will probably need to rely on the command line:

- Almost any time something goes wrong

- Remote systems administration

DOI: 10.1201/9781003311997-5

- Features not supported by GUI

- Scripted tasks

- GUI is broken or not installed

Ubuntu is the widespread Debian-based distribution of the Linux operating system initially released in 2004. Due to its unique features, various distributors of Linux are based in Ubuntu. It is developed and maintained by Canonical Foundation Ltd., which is a large community of software developers around the globe; it is a software company that has its origin in the UK. There are various releases of Ubuntu, such as stable, Long Term Support, and unstable release.

The latest LTS release is 20.04 and will be available till 2025. Ubuntu supports both (CLI) command line interface (CLI) and graphical user interface (GUI) to perform various tasks on the OS. CLI is the primary way to interact with systems hardware (processor/memory); you can perform all GUI's tasks. This chapter will explain the use of various basic commands that provide ease to execute multiple functions of Ubuntu using CLI.

WHAT IS CLI?

It is a powerful program. Beginners are unwilling to use it, considering it is only for advanced users. However, this is not the case.

The command-line interface is referred to as CLI. It's an application that lets users send text instructions into the computer to tell it what to do.

In this whole chapter, you will learn everything you need to know about CLI.

Roots of CLI

In the 1960s, CLI was in use.

People have only a keyboard as an input device, and the computer screen could only display text information. The CLI was the standard user interface in operating systems like MS-DOS.

Users need to type a command on the CLI window to perform tasks, and this is the only method to communicate with the computer.

After typing a command, the users get the result either in a piece of text information or specific action performed by the system. That being said, typing the correct command is the key.

If users enter the wrong command, they will have a chance to delete the files or close the program before saving work – everyone considers this as the main drawback of using CLI.

Then, after years of using a keyboard to the command line, the mouse was invented. The mouse marked the point-and-click method as a new way to interact with any system. This strategy is safer for users, removing them from the risk of CLI. However, we will discuss why using CLI is preferable later. Apart from that, operating systems began to create a more appealing style of computing, employing graphical user interaction (GUI), which was a wonderful approach of using buttons and menus to represent certain commands.

Today, it has become a common way of computing. Most operating systems still have a combination of CLI and GUI. For example, Mac users can use "cal" in the terminal window or click on a Calendar application to get the same results.

SHELL – THE FOUNDATION BEHIND CLI

It is a user interface responsible for executing and processing all commands on CLI. It reads, interprets, and instructs the commands to perform tasks as requested.

A shell, on the other hand, is a user interface that can administer CLI and serves as a middleman between users and the operating system.

Shell can process a variety of things in practice, including:

- It can work with files and directories.

- It can open and close a program.

- It can manage computer processes.

- It can perform repetitive tasks.

- Among many shell types, the most popular ones are Windows shell for Windows and bash for Linux and macOS.

WHAT ARE THE BASIC COMMANDS OF UBUNTU?

This part contains some basic commands of Ubuntu, so let us start and discuss them. Firstly, you have to open the terminal in Ubuntu; press "ctrl + alt + t" from your keyboard to open the terminal.

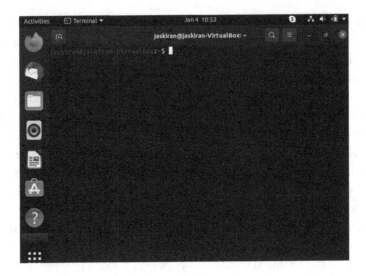

Terminal window.

You will see this window on the screen, and we will discuss some basic Ubuntu Commands that every beginner should know if they are learning Ubuntu for the first time.

Here is a detailed list of basic Ubuntu commands of daily use and safe to use and add sudo before whenever admin privilege is required.

WHAT IS SUDO?

The sudo is a command that allows users to run programs with the security and privileges of another user. The default is the root user.

This section will tell how to create a new user using the Ubuntu systems sudo command. You can use the user account to perform administrative commands without logging in to your Ubuntu server as a root user.

Sudo stands for SuperUser DO. It is used to access restricted files and operations. By default, Linux restricts access to specific system parts controlling sensitive files from being compromised.

The sudo command temporarily elevates privileges allowing users to complete sensitive tasks without logging in as the root user.

Prerequisites

- A system running Linux
- A command line or terminal window then go to Activities > Search > Terminal.
- A user account with root privileges

HOW TO USE THE SUDO COMMANDS

sudo was designed as that way to grant a user administrative privileges temporarily. To make it work, use sudo before a restricted command. The system prompts for the password. Once provided, the system runs the command.

Syntax

Use the following syntax to start using sudo:

$ sudo [command]

For example:

```
sudo -V | -h | -l | -v | -k | -K | -s | [-H]  [-P]  [-S]  [-b] |
[-p prompt]  [-c class|-]  [-a auth_type]  [-r role]  [-t
type]
[-u username|uid]  commandsudo -V | -h | -l | -L | -v | -k | -K |
-s | [-H]  [-P]  [-S]  [-b] |
[-p prompt]  [-c class|-]  [-a auth_type]  [-r role]  [-t
type]
[-u username|#uid]  command
```

When you use the sudo command, a timestamp is entered in the system logs. The user can quickly run commands with elevated privileges (by default, 15 minutes).

OPTIONS

Sudo can use with additional options:

1. **-h – means help**: It displays syntax and command options.

2. **-V – means the version**: It shows the current version of the sudo application.

3. **-v – means validate**: It refreshes the time limit on sudo without running a command.

4. **-l – means the list**: It lists the user's privileges or checks a specific command.

5. **-k – means kill**: It ends the current sudo privileges.

You can get various additional options under the -h option.

```
jaskiran@jaskiran-VirtualBox:~$ sudo -h
sudo - execute a command as another user

usage: sudo -h | -K | -k | -V
usage: sudo -v [-AknS] [-g group] [-h host] [-p prompt] [-u user]
usage: sudo -l [-AknS] [-g group] [-h host] [-p prompt] [-U user] [-u user]
            [command]
usage: sudo [-AbEHknPS] [-r role] [-t type] [-C num] [-g group] [-h host] [-p
            prompt] [-T timeout] [-u user] [VAR=value] [-i|-s] [<command>]
usage: sudo -e [-AknS] [-r role] [-t type] [-C num] [-g group] [-h host] [-p
            prompt] [-T timeout] [-u user] file ...

Options:
  -A, --askpass                 use a helper program for password prompting
  -b, --background              run command in the background
  -B, --bell                    ring bell when prompting
  -C, --close-from=num          close all file descriptors >= num
  -E, --preserve-env            preserve user environment when running command
      --preserve-env=list       preserve specific environment variables
  -e, --edit                    edit files instead of running a command
  -g, --group=group             run command as the specified group name or ID
  -H, --set-home                set HOME variable to target user's home dir
  -h, --help                    display help message and exit
  -h, --host=host               run command on host (if supported by plugin)
  -i, --login                   run login shell as the target user; a command
                                may also be specified
  -K, --remove-timestamp        remove timestamp file completely
  -k, --reset-timestamp         invalidate timestamp file
```

Sudo command help.

EXAMPLES OF SUDO IN LINUX

To execute the following command, then open a terminal window,

$ sudo apt-get update

Enter your password when asked then the system executes the command.

```
jaskiran@jaskiran-VirtualBox:~$ sudo apt-get update
[sudo] password for jaskiran:
Hit:1 http://in.archive.ubuntu.com/ubuntu focal InRelease
Hit:2 http://in.archive.ubuntu.com/ubuntu focal-updates InRelease
Hit:3 http://in.archive.ubuntu.com/ubuntu focal-backports InRelease
Hit:4 http://security.ubuntu.com/ubuntu focal-security InRelease
Hit:5 https://dl.google.com/linux/chrome/deb stable InRelease
Reading package lists... Done
```

Sudo apt-get update command.

To run a command as a separate user, in the terminal window, enter the following command:

Syntax – whoami

For example:

```
jaskiran@jaskiran-VirtualBox:~$ whoami
jaskiran
```

The system should display your username. Next, run the following command:

Syntax – sudo -u [different_username] whoami

For example:

```
jaskiran@jaskiran-VirtualBox:~$ sudo -u root whoami
root
```

SWITCH TO ROOT USER

The command switches your entered command prompt to the BASH shell as a root user:

```
$ sudo bash
```

Your command line changed to:

```
$ root@hostname:/home/[username]
```

For example:

```
jaskiran@jaskiran-VirtualBox:~$ sudo bash
root@jaskiran-VirtualBox:/home/jaskiran#
```

The hostname will be the network name of the particular system—the name of the user that is currently logged in.

RUN MULTIPLE COMMANDS IN ONE LINE

You can add multiple string commands together, separated by a semicolon:

```
$ sudo ls; whoami;
```

```
jaskiran@jaskiran-VirtualBox:~$ sudo ls; whoami
Desktop google-chrome-stable_current_amd64.deb Public
Templates
Documents Music snap Videos
Downloads Pictures Steam
jaskiran
```

ADD A TEXT TO AN EXISTING FILE

You can add a string or text to a file; usually the name of a software repository is used to add to the source's file without opening the file for editing.
Use the below syntax with echo, Sudo, and tee commands:

echo "string-of-text" | [path_to_file]

For example:

```
jaskiran@jaskiran-VirtualBox:~$ cd Desktop
jaskiran@jaskiran-VirtualBox:~/Desktop$ mkdir ubuntu
jaskiran@jaskiran-VirtualBox:~/Desktop$ cd ubuntu
jaskiran@jaskiran-VirtualBox:~/Desktop/ubuntu$ touch
ubuntu.txt
jaskiran@jaskiran-VirtualBox:~/Desktop/ubuntu$ echo
'This is my first file in ubuntu' >>ubuntu.txt
jaskiran@jaskiran-VirtualBox:~/Desktop/ubuntu$
```

This >> symbol is used to append the text in any file. The above
example is of the adding text in the ubuntu.txt file using command life
interface.

EXPLANATION

In the above code, we change our path to the Desktop then create the folder as Ubuntu using the mkdir command. Now move into
your Ubuntu folder, using cd command create the ubuntu.txt empty
file with touch command, and add your text in it using echo "Your
Text" >> filename.

Other useful commands, such as the following:

- **-V**: The -V (means version) option to print the version number and
exit.

```
jaskiran@jaskiran-VirtualBox:~/Desktop/ubuntu$ sudo -V
Sudo version 1.8.31
Sudoers policy plugin version 1.8.31
Sudoers file grammar version 46
Sudoers I/O plugin version 1.8.31
```

- **ls**: The ls (means list) print out the user's commands on the current host.

```
jaskiran@jaskiran-VirtualBox:~$ sudo ls
Desktop google-chrome-stable_current_amd64.deb Public
Templates
Documents Music snap Videos
Downloads Pictures Steam
```

- **-l**: The -l (means list) option will print out the commands allowed the user on the current host.

```
jaskiran@jaskiran-VirtualBox:~$ sudo -l
Matching Defaults entries for jaskiran on
jaskiran-VirtualBox:
env_reset, mail_badpass,
secure_path=/usr/local/sbin\:/usr/local/bin\:/usr/
sbin\:/usr/bin\:/sbin\:/bin\:/snap/bin
User jaskiran may run the following commands on
jaskiran-VirtualBox:
(ALL : ALL) ALL
```

- **-v**: If given the -v (validate), sudo will update the user's timestamp, prompting for the user's password if necessary.

- **-k**: The -k (kill) is to sudo invalidates the user's timestamp.

- **K**: Like the -k option, the -K (sure kill) is used to remove the user's timestamp entirely.

- **-b**: The -b (background) tells sudo to run the given command in the background.

- **-p**: The -p (prompt) allows you to override the default password prompt and use a custom one.

- % you are expanded to the invoking user's login name.

- %U is expanded to the user's login name, and the command will be run.

- %h is expanded to the hostname without the domain name, and %H is expanded, including the domain name.

- %% are collapsed into a single % character.

- **-n**: Use the -n option shown below, which will execute the command without prompting for the password. It is beneficial to run some of the sudo commands as background jobs.

- **10. -u**: The -u (user) sudo to run the specified command as a user other than root.

- **-s**: The -s (shell) runs the shell specified by the SHELL environment variable.

- **-H**: The -H (HOME) sets the HOME environment variable to the target user's home directory.

- The -S (stdin) reads the password from standard input instead of the terminal device.

- **-a**: The -a (authentication type) causes sudo to use the specified authentication type when validating the user.

- **–**: The — flag indicates that sudo stops processing command line arguments and is most useful in conjunction with the -s flag.

WHAT'S A SNAP PACKAGE ON LINUX?

"Snap" refers to the snap command and installation file. It bundles an application and all dependents into one compressed file. The dependents can be library files, web or database servers to launch and run.

Syntax of snap is given below:

$ sudo [Options]

There are various Snap command examples in Linux.

CHECK SNAP VERSION

To check the snap version, you need to use the snap --version command below.

Syntax:

$ snap --version

```
jaskiran@jaskiran-VirtualBox:~/Desktop$ snap --version
snap 2.53.4
snapd 2.53.4
series 16
ubuntu 20.04
kernel 5.11.0-43-generic
```

INSTALL A SNAP

If you want to install a snap, you need to use the snap install <snap_name> syntax. We install a postman using the snap install postman command in this example, as shown below.

For example:

```
jaskiran@jaskiran-VirtualBox:~/Desktop$ snap install
postman
postman (v8/stable) 8.12.5 from Postman, Inc.
(postman-inc*) installed
```

UPDATE A SNAP

If you would like to update a snap to the latest version, you need to use snap refresh <snap_name> syntax. In this example, we update chromium to the newest version using the snap refresh chromium command, as shown below.

For example:

```
jaskiran@jaskiran-VirtualBox:~/Desktop$ snap refresh
postman
snap "postman" has no updates available
```

If there is no update available, "snap postman has no updates available" will show.

REMOVE A SNAP

If you want to remove a snap, you need to remove <snap_name> syntax. This example eliminates postman using the snap remove postman command, as displayed below.

For example:

```
jaskiran@jaskiran-VirtualBox:~/Desktop$ snap remove
postman
postman removed
```

TO LIST ALL THE AVAILABLE UPDATES

If you wish to list all the available snap updates, you need to use the snap refresh –list command as shown below.

For example:

```
jaskiran@jaskiran-VirtualBox: snap refresh --list
Name Version Rev Publisher Notes
chromium 91.0.4472.101 1626 canonical* -
```

If all snaps are up to date, then this will show:

```
jaskiran@jaskiran-VirtualBox:~/Desktop$ snap refresh
--list
All snaps up to date.
jaskiran@jaskiran-Virt
jaskiran@jaskiran-VirtualBox:~/Desktop$ snap list
Name Version Rev Tracking Publisher Notes
atom 1.57.0 282 latest/stable snapcrafters classic
bare 1.0 5 latest/stable canonical* base
chromium-ffmpeg 0.1 24 latest/stable canonical* -
core 162.52.1 11993 latest/stable canonical* core
core18 20211028 2253 latest/stable canonical* base
core20 20211129 1270 latest/stable canonical* base
gimp 2.10.28 383 latest/stable snapcrafters -
telegram 3.4.3 3544 latest/stable telegram.desktop -
vlc 3.0.16 2344 latest/stable videolan* -
wordpressdesktop 6.6.0 109 latest/stable snapcrafters -
```

LIST ALL THE INSTALLED SNAPS

Uses the command snap list to list all the installed snaps in your system, as shown below.

There are various channels available through which you can install a Snap. By default, it gets installed from a stable channel when installed a snap. It can be stable, edge, beta and candidate.

In this example, we install postman through multiple other channels. If you want to install a postman through the edge channel, you need to use the snap install --edge postman command as displayed below.

Syntax:

$ snap install –edge postman

```
jaskiran@jaskiran-VirtualBox:~/Desktop$ snap install
--edge postman
postman (v8/edge) 8.12.5 from Postman, Inc. (postman-
inc*) installed
```

If you want to install postman through the beta channel, you need to use the snap install --beta postman command, as shown below.

Syntax:

$ snap install –beta postman

```
jaskiran@jaskiran-VirtualBox:~/Desktop$ snap install
--beta postman
snap "postman" is already installed, see 'snap help
refresh'
```

CHECK ALL THE INFORMATION ABOUT A SNAP

If you want to see complete snap information, you need to use the snap info <snap_name> syntax. In this example, we list all the information about the postman using the snap info postman command, as shown below.

```
jaskiran@jaskiran-VirtualBox:~/Desktop$ snap info
postman
name: postman
summary: API Development Environment
publisher: Postman, Inc. (postman-inc*)
store-URL: https://snapcraft.io/postman
contact: https://www.postman.com/contact-us
license: unset
description: |
Postman is the complete tool chain for API developers,
used by more than
over 3 million developers and 30000 companies
worldwide. It makes working
with APIs faster & easier by supporting developers at
every stage of
their workflow, is available for, Windows, Linux, Mac
OS X, Chrome
users.
```

```
commands:
- postman
snap-id: fFcOtEEF4EdyYb95IUE5Isy28tICYMLf
tracking: v8/edge
refresh-date: today at 13:59 IST
```

ENABLE A SNAP

If you want to enable the disabled snap, you need to use the snap enables <snap_name> syntax. This example enables the disabled snap postman using the snap enables postman command, as shown below.

For example:

```
jaskiran@jaskiran-VirtualBox: snap enable postman
postman enabled
```

Environment Variables

Here is the list of environment variables used by sudo.

Environment Variables	Description
EDITOR Default editor to use in -e (sudoedit) mode if VISUAL is not set	
HOME In -s or -H mode, set to homedir of the target user	
PATH Set to sane value if secure_path sudoers option is set	
SHELL The -s option is used to decide which shell to execute	
SUDO_PROMPT Used as default password prompt	
SUDO_COMMAND Set to command run by sudo	
SUDO_USER Set to login of the user who invoked sudo	
SUDO_GID Set to gid of the user who invoked sudo	
SUDO_PS1 If set, PS1 will set to its value	

(*Continued*)

Environment Variables	Description
USER Set to the user you want to target (root unless the -u option is specified)	
VISUAL In -e (sudoedit) mode, this is the default editor	

PWD COMMAND

PWD stands for Print Working Directory. It refers to the current working directory in which you are operating your terminal is open. To check PWD, run the PWD keyword in your terminal and then hit enter; the command of PWD is written below along with the result of that command.

PWD command has two flags:

1. **pwd -L**: Prints the symbolic path

2. **pwd -P**: Prints the actual path

And the default behavior of /bin/PWD is the same as pwd -P.

The default behavior of Built-in pwd is the same as pwd -L.

PWD command is a built-in shell command and is available on most of the shell – bash, Bourne shell, ksh, zsh, etc.

The basic syntax of PWD:

$ PWD [OPTION]

Various options used with pwd

- **-L (logical)**: Uses PWD from the environment, even if it contains symbolic links.

- **-P (physical)**: It avoids all symbolic links.

- **–help**: It displays this help and exit.

- **–version**: It outputs version information and exit.

```
jaskiran@jaskiran-VirtualBox:~$ pwd
/home/Jaskiran
```

DIR COMMAND

The command dir displays directory of files and directories stored on disk. ls command is used in listing contents in default listing options. By default, the dir lists the files and folders in columns, sorted vertically, and backslash escape sequences represent special characters.

When you execute the dir command and you want to see them, use the -a command-line option. The syntax of the dir command is given below:

$ dir [OPTION] [FILE]

```
jaskiran@jaskiran-VirtualBox:~$ dir
Desktop google-chrome-stable_current_amd64.deb Public
Templates
Documents Music snap Videos
Downloads Pictures Steam
```

To view all files in a directory, including hidden files, use the -a option and include the -l option to format output as a list.

$ dir -a

$ dir -al

To view the index number of every file, use the option -i. The output below shows that the first column shows numbers, and numbers are called inodes.

$ dir –il

You can view all files sizes using the -s option, and if you need to sort the files according to size, use the -S option.

You also need to use the -h option to view the files sizes in a human-readable format.

$ dir –shl

LS COMMAND

ls is one of the commonly used commands in Linux.

Execute ls command with no option to list files and directories in a bare format where we will not view details like file types, size, modified date and time, permission and links, etc.

Syntax:

$ ls

```
jaskiran@jaskiran-VirtualBox:~$ ls
Desktop google-chrome-stable_current_amd64.deb Public
Templates
Documents Music snap Videos
Downloads Pictures Steam
```

The ls supports various flags, and each flag has a specific role in printing the directories or files of the current working directory.

If you want to print the detailed information of the files-directories, then use the "-al" flag is used with the "ls" command.

Here, ls -l will show file or directory, size, date- time, file or folder name and owner of the file, and its permission.

Syntax

$ ls -l

To list every file, including hidden files starting with ".".

Syntax:

$ ls –a

```
jaskiran@jaskiran-VirtualBox:~$ ls -a
. Pictures
...pki
.atom.profile
.bash_history Public
.bash_logout.pulse-cookie
```

```
.bashrc snap
.cache.ssh
.config.steam
Desktop Steam
Documents.steampath
Downloads.steampid
.gnupg.sudo_as_admin_successful
google-chrome-stable_current_amd64.deb Templates
.local.thunderbird
.mozilla Videos
Music
jaskiran@jaskiran-VirtualBox:~$ ls -al
total 87368
drwxr-xr-x 22 jaskiran jaskiran 4096 Jan 4 13:23.
drwxr-xr-x 2 root root 4096 Dec 28 10:13..
drwxrwxr-x 7 jaskiran jaskiran 4096 Jan 1 12:20.atom
-rw------- 1 jaskiran jaskiran 1206 Jan 4 13:25.
bash_history
-rw-r--r-- 1 jaskiran jaskiran 220 Dec 28 10:13.
bash_logout
-rw-r--r-- 1 jaskiran jaskiran 3771 Dec 28 10:13.bas
hrc
drwx------ 20 jaskiran jaskiran 4096 Jan 2 15:38.cache
drwx------ 20 jaskiran jaskiran 4096 Jan 4 13:23.con
fig
drwxr-xr-x 3 jaskiran jaskiran 4096 Jan 4 13:27
Desktop
drwxr-xr-x 2 jaskiran jaskiran 4096 Dec 28 10:38
Documents
drwxr-xr-x 2 jaskiran jaskiran 4096 Dec 28 10:38
Downloads
drwx------ 3 jaskiran jaskiran 4096 Jan 4 11:30.gnupg
-rw-rw-r-- 1 jaskiran jaskiran 89348996 Dec 12 14:00
google-chrome-stable_current_amd64.deb
```

To show the version of ls command, you can check the version using the ls --version.

Syntax:

$ ls --version

To show ls Command Help Page, you can check it using ls --help,
Syntax:

$ ls --help

You can use the -R with ls command to list directory trees.
Syntax:
$ls -R
For example:

```
jaskiran@jaskiran-VirtualBox:~$ ls -R
.:
Desktop google-chrome-stable_current_amd64.deb Public
Templates
Documents Music snap Videos
Downloads Pictures Steam
./Desktop:
ubuntu
./Desktop/ubuntu:
ubuntu.txt
./Documents:
./Downloads:
./Music:
./Pictures:
./Public:
./snap:
```

CD COMMAND

One of the common commands that can change the directories in the terminal is using the "cd" command. For example, the following command change path of the pwd to desktop.

Syntax

$ cd [directory]

For example:

$ cd Desktop

This command has multiple uses: using this command, one can change the present directory to root directory or home directory. When you open a new terminal, you are in the home directory.

Different functionalities of cd command:

cd /

The command changes the directory to the root directory. The root directory is the first in your filesystem hierarchy.

Syntax:

$ cd /

cd ~

The command changes the directory to the home directory.

Syntax:

$ cd ~

cd

The command also works the same as the cd ~ command.

Syntax:

$cd

cd..

The command is used to move to the parent directory of the current directory. It ".." represents the parent directory.

Syntax:

$ cd..

```
jaskiran@jaskiran-VirtualBox:~$ cd Desktop
jaskiran@jaskiran-VirtualBox:~/Desktop$ mkdir ubuntu
jaskiran@jaskiran-VirtualBox:~/Desktop$ cd ubuntu
jaskiran@jaskiran-VirtualBox:~/Desktop/ubuntu$
```

If you want to change the directory path to root, for example, here we are on the Desktop and want to switch to the root directory, then execute the command:

$ cd /

Then you will be out from the Desktop to its root.

```
jaskiran@jaskiran-VirtualBox:~/Desktop$ cd /
jaskiran@jaskiran-VirtualBox:/$
```

TOUCH COMMAND

The touch is a standard command used in the UNIX-Linux operating system, which is used to create, change and modify time-stamps of a file.
Syntax:

$ touch file_name

There are two commands to create a file which is as follows:

1. **Cat**: It is a command used to create the file with the content.

2. **touch**: It is a command to create a file without any content. The file made using the touch command is empty. The command can be used when the user doesn't have data to store at the file creation time.

```
jaskiran@jaskiran-VirtualBox:~/Desktop/ubuntu$ touch
ubuntu.txt
jaskiran@jaskiran-VirtualBox:~/Desktop/ubuntu$ echo
'This is my first file in ubuntu'>>ubuntu.txt
jaskiran@jaskiran-VirtualBox:~/Desktop/ubuntu$ ls
jaskiran@jaskiran-VirtualBox:~/Desktop/ubuntu$ ubuntu
.txt
```

In the code, we have created an empty file named Ubuntu.txt and added some text without opening it. Then we use >> symbol with the file name. echo is used to print the text on the output screen.

TOUCH COMMAND TO CREATE MULTIPLE FILES

The touch command can create multiple numbers of files simultaneously. These files would be empty during creation.
Syntax:

touch File_1 File_2 File_4

touch -a

It is used to change access time only. To change or update the last access or modification times of a file touch -a command is used.
Syntax:

touch -a file_name

touch -c

It is used to check whether a file is created or not. If not created, then don't create it. This command avoids creating files.
Syntax:

touch -c file_name

touch -c-d

It is used to update access and modification time.
Syntax:

touch -c-d filename

touch -m

It is used to change the modification time only. It only updates the last modification time.
Syntax:

touch -m fileName

touch -r

It is used to use the timestamp of another file. Here Doc2 file is updated with the timestamp of File_1.
Syntax:

touch -r second_file first_file

A FILE HAS THREE TIMESTAMPS AS GIVEN BELOW

- **atime - :** The file was last opened by command or application such as cat, vim, or grep and where a of time is access time.

- **mtime – :** The file content was limited last time, where m of mtime its modify time.

- **ctime – :** The last time the file attribute or content changed, the c of time is change time. The feature includes file permissions, file ownership, or file location.

You can use the stat to display the file status, including the timestamps. Syntax:

stat file_name

For example:

```
jaskiran@jaskiran-VirtualBox:~$ cd Desktop
jaskiran@jaskiran-VirtualBox:~/Desktop$ touch text
_file.txt
jaskiran@jaskiran-VirtualBox:~/Desktop$ stat text_file
.txt
File: text_file.txt
Size: 0 Blocks: 0 IO Block: 4096 regular empty file
Device: 805h/2053d Inode: 674491 Links: 1
Access: (0664/-rw-rw-r--) Uid: (1000/jaskiran) Gid:
(1000/jaskiran)
Access: 2022-01-04 16:38:30.840469486+0530
Modify: 2022-01-04 16:38:30.840469486+0530
Change: 2022-01-04 16:38:30.840469486+0530
Birth: -
```

In the above code we just simply, create an empty file Ubuntu.txt and check the state means timestamps of the file.

CAT COMMAND

Cat means concatenate frequently used command in Linux. It can read data from the file and gives the content as output. It can help us to create, view and concatenate files. So let us see frequently used cat commands.

USE THE COMMAND TO VIEW A SINGLE FILE AS FOLLOWS

Syntax:

$cat filename

USE THE COMMAND TO VIEW MULTIPLE FILES AS FOLLOWS

Syntax:

$cat filename1 filename2

USE THE GIVEN COMMAND TO VIEW THE CONTENTS OF A FILE PRECEDING WITH LINE NUMBERS AS FOLLOWS

Syntax:

$cat -n filename

USE THE COMMAND TO CREATE A FILE AS FOLLOWS

Syntax:

$ cat > new_file

```
jaskiran@jaskiran-VirtualBox:~/Desktop$ cat text_file.
txt
The cat ("concatenate") command is frequently used
commands in Linux/Unix-like operating systems. It
allows us to create single or multiple files, view the
content of a file, concatenate files & redirect output
in terminal or files.
```

MKDIR FILE COMMAND

mkdir command allows you to create directories. This command can create numerous directories at once and. Remember, the user must have enough permissions to create a directory in the parent directory, or otherwise 'permission denied' error occur.

Syntax:

$ mkdir [options] [directories]

–HELP

It displays the help-related information and exits.
   Syntax:

   $ mkdir --help

–VERSION

It displays the version number.
   Syntax:

   $ mkdir --version

-V OR –VERBOSE

It displays a message for every directory created.
   Syntax:

   $ mkdir -v [directories]

-P

A flag that enables the command to create parent directories as necessary.
   Syntax:

   $ mkdir -p [directories]

```
jaskiran@jaskiran-VirtualBox:~$ mkdir Ubuntu
jaskiran@jaskiran-VirtualBox:~$ ls
Desktop google-chrome-stable_current_amd64.deb Public
Templates
Documents Music snap Ubuntu
Downloads Pictures
Steam Videos
```

RM COMMAND

It stands for remove and is used to remove objects such as files, directories.
   To be more specific, rm removes references to objects from the filesystem. Default does not remove directories.
   Syntax:

   $ rm [OPTION] [Filename]

There are various options,

-I (INTERACTIVE DELETION)

The -i the command asks the user for confirmation before removing each file. You have to press y to confirm the deletion. Any other vital leaves the file un-deleted.

For example:

$ rm -i text_file.txt

rm: Remove regular empty file "d.txt"? y

$ ls

e.txt

For example:

```
jaskiran@jaskiran-VirtualBox:~$ cd Desktop
jaskiran@jaskiran-VirtualBox:~/Desktop$ ls
textfile3.txt text_file.txt ubuntu
jaskiran@jaskiran-VirtualBox:~/Desktop$ rm textfile3.txt
jaskiran@jaskiran-VirtualBox:~/Desktop$ ls
text_file.txt ubuntu
jaskiran@jaskiran-VirtualBox:~/Desktop$
```

In the above example, we change our Desktop and list all the files and directory using ls command, now execute the rm command to remove any file in example, we removed textfile3.txt and list them again to check it that it happened or not.

–VERSION

It is used to show the version of rm which is currently running on your system.

$ rm --version

```
jaskiran@jaskiran-VirtualBox:~$ rm --version
rm (GNU Coreutils) 8.30
Copyright (C) 2018 Free Software Foundation, Inc.
```

License GPLv3+: GNU GPL version 3.0 or later<https://
gnu.org/licenses/gpl.html>.
This is open-source software, which means you can
modify and redistribute it.
To the extent permissible by law, there is NO
WARRANTY.
It written by Paul Rubin, David MacKenzie, Richard M.
Stallman,
and Jim Meyering.

MKDIR DIRECTORY COMMAND

mkdir command allows you to create directories. This command can create numerous directories at once and. Remember, the user must have enough permissions to create a directory in the parent directory, or otherwise 'permission denied' error occur.

```
jaskiran@jaskiran-VirtualBox:~/Desktop$ mkdir demo
jaskiran@jaskiran-VirtualBox:~/Desktop$ ls
demo text_file.txt ubuntu
jaskiran@jaskiran-VirtualBox:~/Desktop$ rmdir demo
jaskiran@jaskiran-VirtualBox:~/Desktop$ ls
text_file.txt Ubuntu
```

In the above example, we change our Desktop and list all the files and directory using ls command. Now execute the rm command to remove any directory in example, we removed demo directory and list them again to check it that it happened or not.
   Syntax:

   $ mkdir [options] [directories]

–HELP

It displays the help-related information and exits.
   Syntax:

   $ mkdir --help

–VERSION

It displays the version number.
Syntax:

$ mkdir --version

-V OR –VERBOSE

It displays a message for every directory created.
Syntax:

$ mkdir -v [directories]

-P

A flag that enables the command to create parent directories as necessary.
Syntax:

$ mkdir -p [directories]

CAT COMMAND

Cat means concatenate frequently used command in Linux. It can read data from the file and gives the content as output. It can help us to create, view, concatenate files and let us see some frequently used cat commands.

USE THE COMMAND TO VIEW A SINGLE FILE AS FOLLOWS

Syntax:

$cat filename

USE THE COMMAND TO VIEW MULTIPLE FILES AS FOLLOWS

Syntax:

$cat filename1 filename2

USE THE GIVEN COMMAND TO VIEW THE CONTENTS OF A FILE PRECEDING WITH LINE NUMBERS AS FOLLOWS

Syntax:

$cat -n filename

USE THE COMMAND TO CREATE A FILE AS FOLLOWS

Syntax:

$ cat > new_file

The cat command is used for:

- Display text file on screen

- Read text file

- Create a new text file

- File concatenation

- Modifying file

- Combining text files

- Combining binary files

CREATE A FILE WITH CAT COMMAND

To create a file called "txt_file.txt". enter:
Syntax:
cat > txt_file.txt

```
jaskiran@jaskiran-VirtualBox:~/Desktop$ mkdir
new_directory
jaskiran@jaskiran-VirtualBox:~/Desktop$ ls
new_directory new_file.txt text_file.txt ubuntu
jaskiran@jaskiran-VirtualBox:~/Desktop$ cat text_file.
txt new_directory
```

The cat ("concatenate") command is frequently used commands in Linux/Unix-like operating systems. It allows us to create single or multiple files, view the content of a file, concatenate files & redirect output in terminal or files.
cat: new_directory: Is a directory

In above example, we make new_directory, add some data to the text _file.txt

```
jaskiran@jaskiran-VirtualBox:~/Desktop$ mkdir folder1
jaskiran@jaskiran-VirtualBox:~/Desktop$ mkdir folder2
jaskiran@jaskiran-VirtualBox:~/Desktop$ cat folder1
folder2>all
cat: folder1: Is a directory
cat: folder2: Is a directory
jaskiran@jaskiran-VirtualBox:~/Desktop$ mv text_file.
txt new_directory
jaskiran@jaskiran-VirtualBox:~/Desktop$ cd
new_directory
jaskiran@jaskiran-VirtualBox:~/Desktop/new_directory$ ls
text_file.txt
jaskiran@jaskiran-VirtualBox:~/Desktop$ mv text_file.
txt new_directory
jaskiran@jaskiran-VirtualBox:~/Desktop$ cd
new_directory
jaskiran@jaskiran-VirtualBox:~/Desktop/new_directory$
ls
text_file.txt
jaskiran@jaskiran-VirtualBox:~/Desktop/new_directory$
head text_file.txt
1
2
3
4
5
6
7
8
9
10
```

```
jaskiran@jaskiran-VirtualBox:~/Desktop/new_directory$
tail text_file.txt
6
7
8
9
10
11
12
13
14
15
jaskiran@jaskiran-VirtualBox:~/Desktop/new_directory$
uname
Linux
jaskiran@jaskiran-VirtualBox:~/Desktop/new_directory$
uname -a
Linux jaskiran-VirtualBox 5.11.0-43-generic
#47~20.04.2-Ubuntu SMP
Tue Dec 14 11:06:56 UTC 2021 x86_64 x86_64 x86_64 GNU/
Linux
wget https://download.virtualbox.org/virtualbox/6.1.26
/VirtualBox-6.1.26-145957-Win.exe
```

APT-GET UPDATE

The command apt-get update will update your package lists and will not update software. Note that apt-get requires root permission.

For example:

```
jaskiran@jaskiran-VirtualBox:~$ apt-get update
Reading package lists... Done
E: Could not open file /var/lib/apt/lists/lock - open
(13: Permission denied)
E: Unable to lock directory /var/lib/apt/lists/
W: Problem unlinking the file /var/cache/apt/pkgcache
.bin - RemoveCaches (13: Permission denied)
W: Problem unlinking the file /var/cache/apt/
srcpkgcache.bin - RemoveCaches (13: Permission denied)
```

SUDO APT-GET UPDATE COMMAND

- The sudo apt-get update command downloads package from the configured sources.

- The sources defined in /etc/apt/sources.list file and other files are located in /etc/apt/sources.list.d/ directory.a

- You can run the update command, and it downloads the package information. It is helpful to get info on updated packages or their dependencies.

APT-GET UPGRADE

The command apt-get update will download and update installed software. But it will not install or remove other extra packages. If this command is not working try this,

$ sudo apt upgrade.

For example:

```
jaskiran@jaskiran-VirtualBox:~$ sudo apt upgrade
[sudo] password for jaskiran:
Reading package lists... Done
Building dependency tree
Reading state information... Done
Calculating upgrade... Done
The following packages will be upgraded:
alsa-ucm-conf ghostscript ghostscript-x gir1.2-
mutter-6 gir1.2-udisks-2.0
gnome-control-center gnome-control-center-data
gnome-control-center-faces
gnome-shell-extension-desktop-icons libasound2
libasound2-data
libatopology2 libfprint-2-2 libfprint-2-tod1 libgs9
libgs9-common
libmbim-glib4 libmbim-proxy libmm-glib0
libmutter-6-0.................
```

What does the sudo apt-get upgrade command do?

- You can get an updated list of packages.

- You run sudo apt-get upgrade to install upgrades of all packages installed on the system from the sources via sources.list file.

APT-GET DIST-UPGRADE

It is an improved version of the apt-upgrade command. Separated from upgrading existing software packages, it installs and removes packages to some dependencies.

For example:

```
jaskiran@jaskiran-VirtualBox:~/Desktop$ sudo apt-get
dist-upgrade
[sudo] password for jaskiran:
Reading package lists... Done
Building dependency tree
Reading state information... Done
Calculating upgrade... Done
The following packages were installed and are no
longer required:
linux-headers-5.11.0-27-generic
linux-hwe-5.11-headers-5.11.0-27
linux-image-5.11.0-27-generic
linux-modules-5.11.0-27-generic
```

APT-GET INSTALL <PACKAGE-NAME>

Using the above commands, you may download and install new packages or software named <package-name>. E.g., run sudo apt-get install in your terminal to install Gimp image manipulation software. Notice the sudo before apt-get.

Here is the use of the apt-get command; installing software from an updated repository.

Use the following command to install a software package:

$ sudo apt-get install "package-name".

Example:

You can install the stable version of the Opera browser by installing the package that we searched above, as follows:

$ sudo apt-get install opera-stable or $ snap install opera

For example:

In the example we using snap install opera you can use any of the command,

```
jaskiran@jaskiran-VirtualBox:~/Desktop$ snap install
opera
opera 82.0.4227.43 from Opera (opera-software*)
installed
```

REMOVE A SOFTWARE FROM YOUR SYSTEM

If you want to remove software from the system, you can use the following apt-get command given below:

$ sudo apt-get remove "package-name".

Example of removing Opera:

$ sudo apt-get remove opera-stable or $ snap remove opera

For example:

```
jaskiran@jaskiran-VirtualBox:~/Desktop$ snap remove
opera
opera removed
```

Suppose you don't like the software. You can get rid by simply running the above command but do not forget to change <package-name> with the real one. It will uninstall the software entirely but not the dependent packages.

APT-GET -F INSTALL

Sometimes, while installing software, it fails due to downloading software itself or dependency. To fix broken installation, run the above command.

For example:

```
jaskiran@jaskiran-VirtualBox:~/Desktop$ Sudo apt-get
-f install
Reading package lists... Done
Building dependency tree....Done
Reading state information... Done
The following packages were installed and are no
longer required:
linux-headers-5.11.0-27-generic
linux-hwe-5.11-headers-5.11.0-27
linux-image-5.11.0-27-generic
linux-modules-5.11.0-27-generic
linux-modules-extra-5.11.0-27-generic
Use 'sudo apt autoremove' to remove.
0 upgraded, 0 installed, 0 to remove and 0 not
upgraded.
```

REINSTALL A SOFTWARE PACKAGE WITH APT

While running any application, sometimes it stops working or goes corrupt. In that case, you can reinstall that application through the apt-get command to resolve the same issue using the command as follows:

$ sudo apt-get install "package-name" – reinstall

Example:

$ sudo apt-get install opera-stable – reinstall

adduser command is used to add a new user to your current system. It allows you to modify the configurations of the user which is to be created. It is the same as the useradd command. The adduser command is much interactive as compared to the useradd command.

INSTALLING ADDUSER COMMAND

To install the adduser tool, use the following command as per your Linux distribution.

In the case of Debian/Ubuntu

$sudo apt-get install adduser

For example:

```
jaskiran@jaskiran-VirtualBox:~/Desktop$ Sudo apt-get
install adduser
[sudo] password for jaskiran:
Reading package lists... Done
Building dependency tree
Reading state information... Done
adduser is already the newest version (3.118ubuntu2).
adduser set to manually installed.
The following packages were installed automatically
and are no longer required:
linux-headers-5.11.0-27-generic
linux-hwe-5.11-headers-5.11.0-27
linux-image-5.11.0-27-generic
linux-modules-5.11.0-27-generic
linux-modules-extra-5.11.0-27-generic
Use 'sudo apt autoremove' to remove them.
0 upgraded, 0 newly installed, 0 to remove and 0 not
upgraded.
jaskiran@jaskiran-VirtualBox:~/Desktop$
```

PASSWD COMMAND

The command passwd is used to change the user account passwords. The root user reserves the privilege to change the password for any user on the system, while a regular user can only change the account password for their account.

Syntax:

passwd [options] [username]

MAN COMMAND

The "man" is a short term for a manual page. It is an interface to view the system's reference manual.

```
jaskiran@jaskiran-VirtualBox:~/Desktop$ man ls
LS(1) User Commands LS(1)
NAME
ls - list directory contents
SYNOPSIS
ls [OPTION]... [FILE]...
```

```
DESCRIPTION
It lists information about the FILEs (the current
directory by default).
It sorts entries alphabetically if none of -cftuvSUX
nor --sort is speci-
fied.
It is mandatory arguments to long options are
mandatory for short options
too.
-a, --all
It do not ignore entries starting with.
-A, --almost-all
do not list implied. and..
--author
with -l, print the author of each file
-b, --escape
print C-style escapes for nongraphic characters
```

By typing man, followed by a space, and then argument, a user can request that a man page be displayed. The argument can be a command, utility, or function. Each of these arguments has a manual page connected with it.

Option with their functionality:

- **man -aw**: It lists all available sections of a command.

- **man -a**: It is to view all man pages of a command.

- **sman -k**: It shows a list of results on a man page containing a key-word match.

- **-f, whatis**: It displays descriptions from the manual page if available.

- **whereis**: It is used to determine the location of a man page

DATE COMMAND

The date is used to display the system date and time. It is also used to set the date and time of the system. By default, the date shows the date in the time zone the operating system is configured. You must be on the root to change the date and time.

Syntax:

date [OPTION] [+FORMAT]

OPTIONS WITH EXAMPLES

date (no option):

The command date displays the present date and time, including the abbreviated day name, month name, day, the time separated by (:) colons, the time zone, and the year.

For example:

```
jaskiran@jaskiran-VirtualBox:~/Desktop$ date
Wednesday 05 January 2022 02:57:41 PM IST
```

-u

It displays the time in GMT(i.e., Greenwich Mean Time)/ UTC(Coordinated Universal Time)time zone.
For example:

```
jaskiran@jaskiran-VirtualBox:~/Desktop$ date -u
Wednesday 05 January 2022 09:30:57 AM UTC
```

-d

You can change the date by using "-d" to operate the system on a specific date.
Syntax: date -d Date_to_operate_system_on
For example:

```
jaskiran@jaskiran-VirtualBox:~/Desktop$ date -d now
Wednesday 05 January 2022 04:24:14 PM IST
jaskiran@jaskiran-VirtualBox:~/Desktop$ date -d
last-Sunday
Sunday 02 January 2022 12:00:00 AM IST
jaskiran@jaskiran-VirtualBox:~/Desktop$ dated tomorrow
Thursday 06 January 2022 04:24:34 PM IST
```

CAL COMMAND

Cal is the command for you if you want a view of the calendar. By default, the cal command shows the current month calendar as output. Cal command is a calendar command in Linux used to see the calendar of a specific month or a whole year.

Syntax:

cal [[month] year]

The big brackets mean it is optional.

Various options
cal:
It shows the current month calendar on the terminal with the current date highlighted.
For example:

```
jaskiran@jaskiran-VirtualBox:~/Desktop$ cal
January 2022
Su Mo Tu We Th Fr Sa
                1
2  3  4  5  6  7  8
9  10 11 12 13 14 15
16 17 18 19 20 21 22
23 24 25 26 27 28 29
30 31
```

cal -y :
It shows the calendar of the current year with the current date highlighted.
cal 08 2000 :
It shows the calendar of selected months and years.
For example:

```
jaskiran@jaskiran-VirtualBox:~/Desktop$ cal 11 1998
November 1998
Su Mo Tu We Th Fr Sa
1  2  3  4  5  6  7
8  9  10 11 12 13 14
15 16 17 18 19 20 21
22 23 24 25 26 27 28
29 30
```

cal 2018:
It shows the whole calendar of the year.

WGET COMMAND IN LINUX/UNIX

- wget is the non-interactive network downloader used to download files from the server.

- wget can follow links in the HTML and XHTML pages and make local versions of remote websites.

- wget designed for robustness over slow or unstable network connections.

- wget is non-interactive, means that it can work in the background while the user is not logged on.

- wget is a free tool for downloading files from the internet. It supports FTP protocols, HTTP, HTTPS, as well as HTTP proxy retrieval.

Syntax:

wget [option] [URL]

PING IN UBUNTU

PING (stands Packet Internet Groper) command checks the network connectivity between host and server/host. This command inputs the IP address or the URL and sends a data packet to the specified address with the message "PING", and gets a response from the server/host.

For example:

```
jaskiran@jaskiran-VirtualBox:~/Desktop$ ping -V
ping from iputils s20190709
```

CLEAR COMMAND

Clear is a standard command used to clear the terminal screen, and it is almost similar to the cls command on several other operating systems.

Syntax:

$clear

EXIT COMMAND

It is used to exit the shell where it is currently running. It takes one more parameter as [N] and exits the shell with a return of status N. If n is not provided, it simply returns the status of the last command that is executed.
Syntax:

exit [n]

exit –help: It displays helpful information.

UPTIME COMMAND

The command "uptime" gives information about how long the system has been running in one line. The result will include the current time, the time duration the system has been running, the number of users currently logged on, and the system load for the past 1, 5, and 15 minutes.
Syntax: uptime
For example:

```
jaskiran@jaskiran-VirtualBox:~/Desktop$ uptime
16:26:42 up 4:34, 1 user, load average: 0.19, 0.10,
0.06
```

W COMMAND

The command "w" displays detailed information about the users who are logged in the system currently.
For example:

```
jaskiran@jaskiran-VirtualBox:~/Desktop$ w
16:30:07 up 4:37, 1 user, load average: 0.01, 0.06,
0.05
USER TTY FROM LOGIN@ IDLE JCPU PCPU WHAT
jaskiran :0 :0 10:04 ?xdm? 12:09 0.03s /usr/lib/gdm3/
```

SHUTDOWN COMMAND

The "shutdown" is used to shut down the system.
Syntax: shutdown

MV COMMAND

The command "mv" is used in two ways:

- To move files or directories from one to another path in the system

- To alter the name of a file or folder

"mv" to Move Files

Syntax: mv Source_File Destination_File

For example:

```
jaskiran@jaskiran-VirtualBox:~/Desktop$ touch file1
jaskiran@jaskiran-VirtualBox:~/Desktop$ mkdir folder1
jaskiran@jaskiran-VirtualBox:~/Desktop$ touch file2
jaskiran@jaskiran-VirtualBox:~/Desktop$ mv file1 folder1
jaskiran@jaskiran-VirtualBox:~/Desktop$ cd folder1
jaskiran@jaskiran-VirtualBox:~/Desktop/folder1$ ls
file1
```

In the above example, we create two files with one directory and move the file1 in the directory, and we use the cd command to move inside the folder and execute the ls command to check the move is moved inside it or not.

CP COMMAND

The "cp" is used to copy data from a source to the destination file, almost like "mv".

Syntax: cp source_file_name destination_file_name

For example:

```
jaskiran@jaskiran-VirtualBox:~/Desktop/folder1$ cat
file1
First file data
jaskiran@jaskiran-VirtualBox:~/Desktop/folder1$ cat
fil2
cat: fil2: No such file or directory
jaskiran@jaskiran-VirtualBox:~/Desktop/folder1$ cat
file2
Second file data
jaskiran@jaskiran-VirtualBox:~/Desktop/folder1$ cp
file1 file2
jaskiran@jaskiran-VirtualBox:~/Desktop/folder1$ cat
file2
First file data
```

ECHO COMMAND

The command "echo" displays any expression that is passed as an argument.

Syntax:

echo expression

For example:

```
jaskiran@jaskiran-VirtualBox:~/Desktop/folder1$ echo
"Demo content"
Demo content
```

GREP COMMAND

The command "grep" searches for text in the specified file/folder.
Syntax: grep "expression_to_be_Searched" file_name_to_search_in
For example:

```
jaskiran@jaskiran-VirtualBox:~/Desktop/folder1$ cat
file1
First file data
jaskiran@jaskiran-VirtualBox:~/Desktop/folder1$ grep
"file" file1
First file data
```

In the above example, the text will highlight in red color if it is exists in the file content.

UNZIP COMMAND

The command "unzip" decompresses a .zip file and extracts all the files within to current directory.
Syntax: unzip file_name.zip
For Example:

unzip Files.zip

HISTORY COMMAND

The command "history" displays the list of all commands executed since the user started the session.

Syntax: history

```
jaskiran@jaskiran-VirtualBox:~/Desktop/folder1$
history
 1 wget https://dl.google.com/linux/direct/google-
   chrome-stable_current_amd64.deb
 2 sudo snap install vlc
 3 sudo snap install atom-classic
 4 sudo snap install atom
 5 sudo apk install atom
 6 sudo apt install atom
 7 sudo apt install atom-classic
 8 sudo snap install atom --classic
 9 clear
10 sudo snap install atom --classic
11 sudo snap install gimp
12 sudo apt install franz
13 sudo apt install franz_.5.7.0_and64.deb
14 sudi -h
15 sudo -h
16 whoami
```

whereis

The "whereis" is self-explanatory, as it displays the path where the package for specific built-in Linux command locates.

Syntax: whereis command_name

Example:
  whereis zip

```
jaskiran@jaskiran-VirtualBox:~/Desktop/folder1$
whereis zip
zip: /usr/bin/zip /usr/share/man/man1/zip.1.gzjaskira
n@jaskiran-
```

whereis help

```
jaskiran@jaskiran-VirtualBox:~/Desktop/folder1$
whereis help
help: /usr/share/help
```

whereis cat

```
jaskiran@jaskiran-VirtualBox:~/Desktop/folder1$
whereis cat
cat: /usr/bin/cat /usr/share/man/man1/cat.1.gz
```

whatis

The "whatis" is also self-explanatory, as it displays a brief description of what is command the functionality of specific built-in Linux command.

Syntax: whatis command_name

Example:

whatis cat

```
jaskiran@jaskiran-VirtualBox:~/Desktop/folder1$ whatis
cat
cat - it concatenate files and print on the standard
output
```

whatis help

```
jaskiran@jaskiran-VirtualBox:~/Desktop/folder1$ whatis
help
help: nothing appropriate.
```

whatis zip

```
jaskiran@jaskiran-VirtualBox:~/Desktop/folder1$ whatis
zip
zip (1) - package and compress (archive) files
```

CHMOD COMMAND IN UBUNTU

In Ubuntu LTS, the chmod command is used to change the access mode of any file. It is an abbreviation of change mode.

Change of mode or chmod command lets you change the access mode of files in Linux. It enables you to decide who can access and run files.

Now we are going to discuss some of the Ubuntu permissions commands.

VIEW FILES PERMISSIONS

To view the permissions for a file, use the command given below:

$ ls –l

```
For example, jaskiran@jaskiran-VirtualBox:~$ ls -l
total 87304
drwxr-xr-x 3 jaskiran jaskiran 4096 Jan 5 16:41
Desktop
drwxr-xr-x 2 jaskiran jaskiran 4096 Dec 28 10:38
Documents
drwxr-xr-x 2 jaskiran jaskiran 4096 Dec 28 10:38
Downloads
-rw-rw-r-- 1 jaskiran jaskiran 0 Jan 5 10:59 fil1.txt
-rw-rw-r-- 1 jaskiran jaskiran 0 Jan 5 10:59 fil2.txt
-rw-rw-r-- 1 jaskiran jaskiran 89348996 Dec 12 14:00
google-chrome-stable_current_amd64.deb
drwxr-xr-x 2 jaskiran jaskiran 4096 Dec 28 10:38 Music
drwxr-xr-x 2 jaskiran jaskiran 4096 Dec 28 10:38
Pictures
drwxr-xr-x 2 jaskiran jaskiran 4096 Dec 28 10:38
Public
drwx------ 11 jaskiran jaskiran 4096 Jan 4 11:47 snap
drwxrwxr-x 3 jaskiran jaskiran 4096 Dec 31 22:31 Steam
drwxr-xr-x 2 jaskiran jaskiran 4096 Dec 28 10:38
Templates
drwxrwxr-x 2 jaskiran jaskiran 4096 Jan 4 17:05 Ubuntu
drwxr-xr-x 2 jaskiran jaskiran 4096 Dec 28 10:38
Videos
```

There are three user types:

1. **Owner**: This is the user who owns the file.

2. **Group**: These are users who are part of a user group.

3. **Others**: These are users other than the owner and group members.

USER PERMISSIONS IN LINUX

There are three basic permissions given below:

- **read (r)**: It means the user can only read or view the file.

- **write (w)**: It allows users to edit or delete a file.

- **execute (x)**: It will enable users to run the file.

The permissions are represented as characters or –. The "–" (dash) means the users do not have permission.

CHMOD SYNTAX

The syntax of chmod is given below:

$ chmod {users options} {operator} {permission} {filename}

Various operators let you specify the permissions.

There are three different operators used in chmod command:

1. +: Adds the permission.

2. -: Removes the permission.

3. =: Let's you specify the explicit permission.

chmod command modifies the file's permissions specified by filename to the permissions set by Permissions.

Permissions define the permissions for the owner of the file ("user"), members of the group which owns the file ("group"), and ("others").

There are two methods to represent these permissions:

1. Using symbols (alphanumeric characters)

2. Octal numbers (the digits 0 through 7)

If you are the owner of a file named my_file, and you can set its permissions so that:

- You can read, write, and execute it.

- Members of the group can read and run it, and others can only read it.

- The command does the trick:

   chmod u=rwx,g=rx,o=r myfile

The digits 7, 5, and 4 each represent the user's, group's, and others' permissions in the same order. Each digit is a combination of the 4, 2, 1, and 0 digit numbers:

- 4 stands for "read"
- 2 stands for "write"
- 1 stand for "execute"
- 0 stands for "no permission"

Setting and Modifying Permissions

Suppose you have a file and check full permissions on it.

    ls -l new_ file.txt

For example:

```
jaskiran@jaskiran-VirtualBox:~/Desktop$ ls -l new_file
.txt
-rw-rw-r-- 1 jaskiran jaskiran 0 Jan 7 11:29 new_file.
txt
```

These are some files in the current directory:

    ls -l

```
jaskiran@jaskiran-VirtualBox:~/Desktop$ ls -l
total 4
drwxrwxr-x 2 jaskiran jaskiran 4096 Jan 5 16:43
folder1
-rw-rw-r-- 1 jaskiran jaskiran 0 Jan 7 11:29 new_file.
txt
```

kill

It is a process of specifying its PID, either via a signal or forced termination.
Syntax

- kill PID
- kill -l [exit_status]
- kill -l [sigspec]

Key

- -l List the signal names

- -s Send a specific signal

- -n Send a specific signal number

For example:

```
jaskiran@jaskiran-VirtualBox:~/Desktop$ kill
kill: usage: kill [-s sigspec|-n signum|-sigspec]
pid|jobspec... or kill -l [sigspec]
```

CHAPTER SUMMARY

In this chapter, we had a brief discussion on the CLI and some basic commands of the Ubuntu system with examples.

Bibliography

@snapcraftio. (n.d.). *Install Audacity on Ubuntu using the Snap Store*. Snapcraft. Retrieved July 9, 2022, from https://snapcraft.io/install/audacity/ubuntu

@snapcraftio. (n.d.). *Install Google Play Music Desktop Player on Linux*. Snap Store. Retrieved July 9, 2022, from https://snapcraft.io/google-play-music -desktop-player

@snapcraftio. (n.d.). *Install notepadqq on Ubuntu using the Snap Store*. Snapcraft. Retrieved July 9, 2022, from https://snapcraft.io/install/notepadqq/ubuntu

@snapcraftio. (n.d.). *Install Picard on Ubuntu using the Snap Store*. Snapcraft. Retrieved July 9, 2022, from https://snapcraft.io/install/picard/ubuntu

@snapcraftio. (n.d.). *Install Pixbuf on Ubuntu using the Snap Store*. Snapcraft. Retrieved July 9, 2022, from https://snapcraft.io/install/pixbuf-desktop/ ubuntu

@snapcraftio. (n.d.). *Install Sayonara on Ubuntu using the Snap Store*. Snapcraft. Retrieved July 9, 2022, from https://snapcraft.io/install/sayonara/ubuntu

@snapcraftio. (n.d.). *Install Shotcut on Ubuntu using the Snap Store*. Snapcraft. Retrieved July 9, 2022, from https://snapcraft.io/install/shotcut/ubuntu#:~ :text=Shotcut%20is%20a%20free%2C%20open,and%20resolution%20sup-port%20to%204k

@snapcraftio. (n.d.). *Install Speedy Duplicate Finder on Ubuntu using the Snap Store*. Snapcraft. Retrieved July 9, 2022, from https://snapcraft.io/install/ speedy-duplicate-finder/ubuntu

@thegadgetmonkey. (2019, December 11). *Ubuntu Desktop vs. Ubuntu Server: What's the Difference?* MUO. https://www.makeuseof.com/tag/differ-ence-ubuntu-desktop-ubuntu-server/#:~:text=The%20main%20difference %20between%20Ubuntu,because%20most%20servers%20run%20headless

340.2. *What is GNU/Linux?* (n.d.). Retrieved July 9, 2022, from https://www .debian.org/releases/buster/amd64/ch01s02.en.html

AM, & Sandi. (2020, October 22). *How to Install WordPress Desktop Client on Ubuntu 20.04*. ImagineLinux. https://www.imaginelinux.com/install -wordpress-desktop-client-on-ubuntu-20-04/

Brown, K. (2021, April 13). *Linux Tutorials – Learn Linux Configuration*. PDF Viewer List on Ubuntu 22.04 Jammy Jellyfish Linux. https://linuxconfig .org/pdf-viewer-list-on-ubuntu-22-04-jammy-jellyfish-linux

Brown, K. (2021, April 23). *Linux Tutorials – Learn Linux Configuration.* How to Install Fonts on Ubuntu 20.04 Focal Fossa Linux. https://linuxconfig.org/how-to-install-fonts-on-ubuntu-20-04-focal-fossa-linux

Buzdar, K. (2021, August 17). *Install Tilix Terminal Emulator in Ubuntu.* LinuxWays. https://linuxways.net/ubuntu/install-tilix-terminal-emulator-in-ubuntu/

Buzdar, K. (2021, December 20). *How to Install Geary Email Client on Ubuntu 20.04.* LinuxWays. https://linuxways.net/ubuntu/how-to-install-geary-email-client-on-ubuntu-20-04/

Buzdar, K. (2021, October 15). *How to Install Terminator on Ubuntu 20.04.* LinuxWays. https://linuxways.net/centos/how-to-install-terminator-on-ubuntu-20-04/

Buzdar, K. (2021, October 30). *How to Install Franz Messenger on Ubuntu 20.04 LTS.* LinuxWays. https://linuxways.net/ubuntu/how-to-install-franz-messenger-on-ubuntu-20-04-lts/

Das, A. (2021, April 16). *Foliate: A Modern eBook Reader App for Linux.* It's FOSS. https://itsfoss.com/foliate-ebook-viewer/

Desktop Environment - Wikipedia. (2012, February 4). https://en.wikipedia.org/wiki/Desktop_environment. Last edited on August 21, 2022.

Difference between Ubuntu Desktop and Ubuntu Server. (n.d.). Retrieved July 9, 2022, from https://linuxhint.com/ubuntu-desktop-ubuntu-server-difference/

Flatpak—The Future of Application Distribution. (n.d.). Retrieved July 9, 2022, from https://flatpak.org/setup/Ubuntu

The History of Linux and Ubuntu. (2020, May 18). Answertopia. https://www.answertopia.com/ubuntu/the-history-of-linux-and-ubuntu/#:~:text=The%20source%20code%20that%20makes,Debian%20created%20by%20Ian%20Murdoch

History of Linux - Wikipedia. (2015, March 15). https://en.wikipedia.org/wiki/History_of_Linux. Last edited on September 22, 2022.

How to Burn an .iso Image onto a CD/DVD-ROM | Seagate Support US. (n.d.). Retrieved July 9, 2022, from https://www.seagate.com/in/en/support/kb/how-to-burn-an-iso-image-onto-a-cddvd-rom-201431en/

How to Create a Bootable USB Disk from Ubuntu Terminal?. (2020, May 31). LinuxForDevices. https://www.linuxfordevices.com/tutorials/ubuntu/create-ate-bootable-usb-disk-ubuntu-terminal

How to Dual-Boot Linux and Windows. (n.d.). Opensource.Com. Retrieved July 9, 2022, from https://opensource.com/article/18/5/dual-boot-linux

How to Install Clementine Music Player on Ubuntu 22.04. (n.d.). Retrieved July 9, 2022, from https://linuxhint.com/clementine-music-player-linux/

How to Install Corebird Twitter Client 1.5.1 on Ubuntu 17.04 and Below. (n.d.). Retrieved July 9, 2022, from https://linuxhint.com/install-corebird-twitter-client-linux/

How to Install Krita in Ubuntu 20.04. (n.d.). Retrieved July 9, 2022, from https://linuxhint.com/install_krita_ubuntu/#:~:text=To%20install%20the%20AppImage%20of,download%20Krita%20onto%20your%20system.&text=Now%2C%20double%2Dclick%20on%20the,prompt%2C%20and%20%20Krita%20will%20start

How to Install Skype on Ubuntu 20.04. (2020, June 7). https://linuxize.com/post/how-to-install-skype-on-ubuntu-20-04/

How to Install Steam in Ubuntu 20.04. (n.d.). Retrieved July 9, 2022, from https://linuxhint.com/install-steamos-on-ubuntu/

How to Install the Tweak Tool in Ubuntu 20.10? (n.d.). Retrieved July 9, 2022, from https://linuxhint.com/unity-tweak-tool-ubuntu/#:~:text=Tweak%20tools%20are%20used%20to,desktop%20environment%20for%20several%20years

How to Install VLC Media Player on Ubuntu 20.04. (n.d.). Retrieved July 9, 2022, from https://linuxhint.com/install_vlc_media_player_ubuntu/#:~:text=To%20launch%20the%20Snap%20Store,click%20on%20the%20VLC%20icon

How to Manage Packages in Ubuntu and Debian with Apt-Get & Apt-Cache. (2013, August 6). DigitalOcean. https://www.digitalocean.com/community/tutorials/how-to-manage-packages-in-ubuntu-and-debian-with-apt-get-apt-cache

https://assets.ubuntu.com/v1/f954307f-ubuntu-server-guide.pdf

https://www.linuxcapable.com/how-to-install-gimp-on-ubuntu-20-04/

IN, D. (n.d.). *Introduction to Basic Troubleshooting Commands within Ubuntu Linux.* Dell India. Retrieved July 9, 2022, from https://www.dell.com/support/kbdoc/en-in/000123974/introduction-to-basic-troubleshooting-commands-within-ubuntu-linux

Install Guake Terminal on Ubuntu and Mint Linux. (2014, March 9). LinTut. https://lintut.com/how-to-install-guake-on-ubuntu-and-mint-linux/#:~:text=Installing%20Guake&text=If%20you%20want%20Guake%20available,Guake%20as%20a%20startup%20application

Install Latest Telegram Desktop Messenger App on Ubuntu 22.04. (n.d.). Retrieved July 9, 2022, from https://linuxhint.com/install-telegram-desktop-messenger-linux/?nowprocket=1

Installation/FromUSBStick - Community Help Wiki. (n.d.). Retrieved July 9, 2022, from https://help.ubuntu.com/community/Installation/FromUSBStick

Installation/SystemRequirements - Community Help Wiki. (n.d.). Retrieved July 9, 2022, from https://help.ubuntu.com/community/Installation/SystemRequirements

Is Ubuntu Beginner Friendly? (n.d.). Quora. Retrieved July 9, 2022, from https://www.quora.com/Is-Ubuntu-beginner-friendly

Ivankov, A. (2020, June 23). *Ubuntu Operating System: Advantages and Disadvantages.* Profolus. https://www.profolus.com/topics/ubuntu-operating-system-advantages-and-disadvantages/

Johorcse. (n.d.). *Unixmen-Linux/Unix News and Reviews.* How to Install Mumble Server on Ubuntu. Retrieved July 9, 2022, from https://www.unixmen.com/install-mumble-server-ubuntu/

Khera, G. (2021, May 19). *13 Open Source LightWeight Desktop Environments I Discovered in 2015.* https://www.tecmint.com/top-best-linux-lightweight-desktop-environments/

Kili, A. (2020, October 22). *How to Install Shutter Screenshot Tool in Ubuntu 20.04.* https://www.tecmint.com/install-shutter-in-ubuntu/

KL, A. (2021, November 2). *Introduction to Ubuntu*. The Sec Master. https://thesecmaster.com/introduction-to-ubuntu/

Maurya, H. (2022, January 5). *3 Ways to Install Inkscape on Ubuntu 20.04 | 22.04 LTS*. Linux Shout. https://www.how2shout.com/linux/3-ways-to-install-inkscape-on-ubuntu-20-04-22-04-lts/

Microsoft Windows - Wikipedia. (2022, May 1). https://en.wikipedia.org/wiki/Microsoft_Windows. Last edited on October 4, 2022.

Package Management. (n.d.). Ubuntu. Retrieved July 9, 2022, from https://ubuntu.com/server/docs/package-management

Prakash, A. (2020, March 18). *How to Install Pinta on Ubuntu & Linux Mint*. It's FOSS. https://itsfoss.com/pinta-1-6-ubuntu-linux-mint/

Prakash, A. (2020, October 29). *How to Install Brave Browser on Ubuntu & Other Linux*. It's FOSS. https://itsfoss.com/brave-web-browser/

Prakash, A. (2020, October 29). *How to Install VirtualBox on Ubuntu Linux [3 Simple Ways]*. It's FOSS. https://itsfoss.com/install-virtualbox-ubuntu/

Prakash, A. (2020, September 3). *What is Desktop Environment in Linux?* It's FOSS. https://itsfoss.com/what-is-desktop-environment/

Prakash, A. (2021, November 29). *How to Install Google Chrome on Ubuntu Linux [GUI & Terminal]*. It's FOSS. https://itsfoss.com/install-chrome-ubuntu/

Prakash, A. (2021, September 3). *How to Install Dropbox on Ubuntu Linux*. It's FOSS. https://itsfoss.com/install-dropbox-ubuntu/

Rendek, Lubos. (2020, May 13). *Linux Tutorials – Learn Linux Configuration*. How to Install Blender on Ubuntu 20.04 Focal Fossa Linux Desktop. https://linuxconfig.org/how-to-install-blender-on-ubuntu-20-04-focal-fossa-linux-desktop

Rendek, Lubos. (2020, May 13). *Linux Tutorials – Learn Linux Configuration*. How to Install Mailspring on Ubuntu 20.04 Focal Fossa Linux Desktop. https://linuxconfig.org/how-to-install-mailspring-on-ubuntu-20-04-focal-fossa-linux-desktop

Screen Recording with Kazam on Ubuntu. (2019, February 26). VITUX. https://vitux.com/screen-recording-with-kazam-on-ubuntu/

Sneddon, J. (2017, January 4). *The Easy Way to Integrate Your Android Phone with Ubuntu*. OMG! Ubuntu! https://www.omgubuntu.co.uk/2017/01/kde-connect-indicator-ubuntu

The Top 10 Advantages Ubuntu has Over Windows. (2018, March 19). FOSSMint: Everything About Linux and FOSS. https://www.fossmint.com/advantages-ubuntu-has-over-windows/

Tromp, D. (2020, December 26). *How to Install Ubuntu on Your Computer*. TurboFuture. https://turbofuture.com/computers/How-to-Install-Ubuntu-on-your-Computer

Ubuntu - Overview. (n.d.). Retrieved July 9, 2022, from https://www.tutorialspoint.com/ubuntu/ubuntu_overview.htm#:~:text=Ubuntu%20is%20a%20Linux%2Dbased,of%20Open%20Source%20software%20development

Ubuntu - Wikipedia. (2004, October 20). https://en.wikipedia.org/wiki/Ubuntu. Last edited on September 30, 2022.

Ubuntu Desktop Guide. (n.d.). Retrieved July 9, 2022, from https://help.ubuntu
.com/stable/ubuntu-help/

Ubuntu Flavours. (n.d.). Ubuntu. Retrieved July 9, 2022, from https://ubuntu
.com/desktop/flavours

*Ubuntu Promises and Goals | The Official Ubuntu Book, 7th Edition: The Ubuntu
Story.* (n.d.). InformIT. Retrieved July 9, 2022, from https://www.informit
.com/articles/article.aspx?p=2209012&seqNum=5

Unix - Wikipedia. (1971, November 1). https://en.wikipedia.org/wiki/Unix#:~
:text=The%20origins%20of%20Unix%20date,but%20also%20presented
%20severe%20problems. Last edited on October 7, 2022.

What is a Desktop Environment? (n.d.). Retrieved July 9, 2022, from https://www
.computerhope.com/jargon/d/desktop-environment.htm

What is Apt-get Upgrade and Dist-upgrade Commands and How to Use Them.
(n.d.). Retrieved July 9, 2022, from https://linuxhint.com/apt_get_upgrade
_dist_upgrade/?nowprocket=1

What is Ubuntu? - Definition from Techopedia. (n.d.). Retrieved July 9, 2022, from
https://www.techopedia.com/definition/3307/ubuntu

What is Ubuntu? | The Official Ubuntu Book, 7th Edition: The Ubuntu Story.
(n.d.). InformIT. Retrieved July 9, 2022, from https://www.informit.com/
articles/article.aspx?p=2209012&seqNum=4

What Language is the Word "Ubuntu"? (n.d.). Quora. Retrieved July 9, 2022, from
https://www.quora.com/What-language-is-the-word-Ubuntu

ZoomAdmin.com. (n.d.). *How to Install Arora Ubuntu Package on Ubuntu 20.04/
Ubuntu 18.04/Ubuntu 19.04/Ubuntu 16.04.* Retrieved July 9, 2022, from
https://zoomadmin.com/HowToInstall/UbuntuPackage/arora

Index

Printed in the United States
by Baker & Taylor Publisher Services

Printed in the United States
by Baker & Taylor Publisher Services